MASTERS OF EUROPEAN DRAMA

D0561839

By the same author:

MASTERS OF BRITISH DRAMA
GOING TO THE THEATRE
GREAT MOMENTS IN THE THEATRE
PLAY PRODUCTION

MASTERS OF
EUROPEAN DRAMA

by

JOHN ALLEN

The Citadel Press New York

Grateful acknowledgements are made for permission
to quote from the following works: Oxford University Press for Lewis Campbell's translation of
Aeschylus in World's Classics; William Heinemann
Ltd. for Herbert Smyth's translation of Aeschylus in
the Loeb Classical Library; Faber & Faber Ltd. for
Louis Macneice's translation of *Faust*.

First American Edition 1968
Copyright © 1962 by John Allen
All rights reserved
Published by Citadel Press, Inc.
222 Park Avenue South, New York, N. Y. 10003
Manufactured in the United States of America
Library of Congress Catalog Card Number 68-28447

Contents

Illustrations

The following plates are reproduced by courtesy of the Radio Times Hulton Picture Library : IV, VII, VIII, IX, XIII, XIV, XV, XVI.

MASTERS OF EUROPEAN DRAMA

CHAPTER ONE

Reading and Seeing Plays in Translation

I BEGAN my book *Masters of British Drama* with a chapter about reading plays and the importance of seeing the works of the great dramatists on the stage whenever possible. I am not going to repeat myself. This book is about dramatists who did not write in English. So I am going to begin with a few words explaining why I think it is important that people should read and see plays in their original language whenever possible and what they should look for when they read and see plays in translation.

The first thing of course is to acquire an interest in foreign languages. I am afraid that this interest is not always cultivated by the way that languages are taught at school. But there are plenty of excellent language teachers and anyone who really makes up his mind to master a language can hardly fail to discover something fascinating even in conjugations and declensions.

First, we must regard language as a living thing—even so-called 'dead' languages like Latin and Greek. Many of the finest writers, poets, historians, philosophers and dramatists wrote in Greek and, even if Latin literature is not as full of great works as Greek, this was the language spoken every day by the men and women who created one of the most remarkable empires the world has ever seen.

So let us remember that language is a means of expressing ideas. And it's hardly necessary to point out what a futile place the world would become if we lost our interest in ideas. It's possible to argue, of course, that if we didn't have language we wouldn't have ideas. Many anthropologists believe that tens of thousands of years ago when men were evolving rapidly from what they call 'near-men' into homo-sapiens, when our brains were both swelling in size and growing in efficiency, the development of the ability to think went hand-in-hand with the ability to speak, that is, to put thoughts into words. Have we any means of thinking except by putting our thoughts into words in our mind?

If this is true, let us think about the suitability of different languages for expressing thought. 'He loves' in French is 'il aime'. But 'il aime' is the best the French can do for 'he is loving' or 'he does love'. The little monosyllabics add to the richness of the English. In Latin 'he loves' is simply 'amat' : it's simpler still. The French for 'they love' is 'ils aiment' and the Latin 'amant'. In French and Latin the verbs express the change of person, in Latin to the exclusion of the pronoun. Many words in fact change a great deal more in Latin and Greek than they do in French and more in French than in English. Languages in which changes of case, person or tense are shown principally by changes within the word itself are known as inflected languages. Philologists point out, however, that the highly inflected Latin which is taught at school and which was used by classic authors was very different from the language spoken by the Romans.

These examples show that Latin and Greek are more economical languages than French or English but it is open to question whether they are clearer. In fact we find that in more complex sentences Greek is very often clearer, or anyway more precise, than English; but this only goes to show the danger of generalising about a very subtle matter. The point to consider is whether such tiresome grammatical complications as the ablative absolute in Latin, the optative mood in Greek, the occasional use of 'ne' with a subjunctive in

French, and innumerable other vernacular or idiomatic oddities of a similar kind are helpful for ensuring clarity and precision of thought or not.

Another aspect of language that must have struck everyone on learning a foreign tongue is the order of words. What are we to think about the variety that is permissible in Latin and Greek? Does it lead to clarity or confusion? What are we to think about the German custom of placing past participles at the end of the sentence, and in dependant clauses the whole of the verb? Word order is a highly complicated affair in many languages. These idiosyncracies were not incorporated in languages by people who wanted to make them difficult for foreigners to learn!

All this is to suggest that in spite of the horrors of grammar to learn a foreign language may be a fascinating undertaking, quite apart from the pleasure of speaking that language in visiting the country, or reading its literature in the original—a reward that makes the mastery of Greek infinitely rewarding.

But there are two stumbling blocks to learning a foreign language: grammar and vocabulary. Something has been said about the former: what about the vocabulary of a foreign language—its words?

It's possible to tell quite a lot about the people of a country from their vocabulary. Let us have a look at English. How many words are there in English for a row? Contest, war, hostilities, fight, battle, tussle, skirmish, foray, shindy, rumpus . . . there ought to be a word to describe exactly the kind of set-to the speaker or writer wants to describe. How do we fare with words describing the opposite situation? Love, affection, sympathy, understanding, comradeship . . . we don't do quite so well. Is any one of these words adequate to describe a deep emotional relationship between two people? It may be answered that there are many more kinds of quarrel than of human relationships. But is that really so? Or is it that we talk more readily and more exactly about quarrelling than about the gentler relationships between two people. The Australians in settling their vast country found the greatest problem they had to face in the great open spaces was loneliness. Consequently they came to value beyond most other virtues, comradeship. They call it 'mateship', a word of their own creation to describe a unique relationship. And they have a number of other words like 'cobber' and 'digger' which they invented because they found 'friend' and 'comrade' not expressive enough and made stale by over-use.

Now let us compare for a moment words between one language and another. This is a game that everyone can play with the aid of a dictionary or two. Which of these words seems best to describe the silvery planet which is the present object of our spatial physicists? Moon, lune (French), Mond (German—though the spelling does no justice to the lovely sound on native lips), the Dutch maan, or the Greek selina?

I don't want to suggest that the standard by which a language is to be measured is the sensual beauty of its word for the moon. Many people think that the Australians speak English with an accent that does less than justice to the language of Shakespeare and the Jacobean Bible and that American dialects are destructive of the beauties of our tongue. But we must not approach the spoken language with abstract and absolute standards of what constitutes good speech. A living language has two important qualities: a flexible vernacular enabling people to say what they want to say clearly and to the point; and a rich vocabulary providing words with a wide and subtle range of meaning as well as sufficient sonority to carry such shades of emotional meaning as the speaker may care to put into them. I believe that one of the reasons why poets have singled out the nightingale for special praise—for I am sure that few of them have ever heard the bird—in preference to the thrush which is no mean songster, is simply because the word 'nightingale' is an evocative one. I have mentioned the way in which Australians and Americans speak English. They don't make music of the language but they make incomparably clear and vivid sounds highly charged with meaning. I would rather hear the Australians' hearty 'Ow yer doin' mate, oright?' than a limp 'Good morning, how are you?' Even the American habit of using 'uh-huh' with an upward inflection for 'yes' and a downward for 'no' can be singularly expressive.

Words are the material of the dramatist; and few languages have so rich a vocabulary as English. The invaders who made life intolerable for our ancestors in the centuries leading up to the Norman conquest, left a rich legacy in their languages. Romans, Teutons, Norsemen, Saxons, Danes and Normans all settled uninvited in Britain, spoke their own language in preference to learning ours, and left their mark in the wonderful instrument of human speech that was finally perfected by Chaucer and Shakespeare. Our language is living history.

Here by way of example are some quotations to show how our language has developed over the last six hundred years.

First of all a well-known passage from the twenty-third Psalm in a translation by an Augustinian monk called Richard Hampole writing in 1350 or thereabouts.

'Our Lord governeth me, and nothing to me shall want: stede of pasture thar he me set. In the water of the hetyng forth he me broughte: my soul he turnyd. He ladde me on the stretis of rygtwisnesse for his name.
For win gif I hadde goo in myddil of the shadewe of death, I shall not dreede yveles; for thou art with me. Thy gerde and thi stef, thei have comfortid me.'

In this you will have recognised the famous lines:

'The Lord is my shepherd: I shall not want. He maketh me to lie down in green pastures: He leadeth me beside the still waters. He restoreth my soul; he leadeth me in the paths of righteousness for his name's sake.

Yea, though I walk through the valley of the shadow of death I will fear no evil: for thou art with me; thy rod and thy staff they comfort me.'

Those gloriously sensual lines were written in 1611.

Although we don't know how the earlier passage was pronounced, we do know that it was very different from English pronunciation of the twentieth century. It's easy to appreciate its craggy simplicity. 'For win gif I had goo in myddil of the shadewe of death. . . .' is a splendid string of hard monosyllabics, broken only by the one word that has a gentle meaning, 'shadow'. But the man who wrote 'Yea, though I walk through the valley of the shadow of death, I will fear no evil', not only had a fully developed language to use, but was a master in using it, and so in turn developed its scope. The danger of what we have come to call 'purple passages' such as we find in the Authorised version of the Bible and in Shakespeare too is that we are inclined to delight in the sensual and sonorous sound of the words without any regard for their meaning. That way lies hugger-mugger.

The two main ingredients of the English language are the Nordic stream with all its Scandinavian words, and the Romance stream with its Mediterranean words. In the Middle Ages words from the latter source stood out by reason of the large number of people who spoke Norman French, and the universality of Latin. Here is a passage from a play called *Mary Magdalene* which was written about 1400 and in which the dramatist is deliberately using as many words of florid Mediterranean origin as possible in order to create an impression of courtliness and flattery. The scene is one in which Lechery is trying to persuade Mary to have a night out with him in Jerusalem.

Lechery: Heyl, lady most laudabyll of alyauns!
          Heyl, oryent as the sonne in his reflexity!
          Myche pepul be comfortyd by your benyng
            afyauns.
          Bryter than the bornyd is your bemys of bewte;
          Most debonarius with your aungelly delycyte!
Mary: Qwat personne be ye that thus me comende?
Lechery: Your servant to be, I wold comprehende.
Mary: Your debonarius obedyauns ravyssyt me to trank-
            quelyte!

No doubt the dramatist congratulated himself on that last line!

But the writer who first made full harmony out of the English language was Geoffrey Chaucer. Here are the famous opening lines of the *Canterbury Tales* which show his absolute mastery of words:

>   Whan that Aprille with his shoures soote
>   The droghte of March hath perced to the roote
>   And bathed every veyne in swich licour
>   Of which vertu engendered is the flour. . .

This is not easy to read at sight but once mastered the music is unforgettable. Do we really gain very much by modernising these glorious words as a notable English scholar has done?

>   When the sweet showers of April fall and shoot
>   Down through the drought of March to pierce the root,
>   Bathing every vein in liquid power
>   From which there springs the engendering of the flower;

The supreme master of the English language is William Shakespeare. There is no aspect of human nature, there is no mood, thought or emotion, for which he hasn't an exquisite line, from the ravings of the mad Lear to the obscenities of Falstaff, from the rare beauty of *The Winter's Tale* to the heroics of *Henry V*. As a boy at school I was first enthralled in his marvellous use of language by the famous lines in *Macbeth*

> . . . this my little hand will rather
> The multitudinous seas incarnadine
> Making the green one red.

Although we may question the meaning of the last few words, they make a tremendous contrast to the line that precedes them, with 'multitudinous' and 'incarnadine' sharpened by the sibilant 'seas' between them. A word like the Greek 'thalassa' would have destroyed the words on either side of it.

There is hardly a play of Shakespeare's that is not teeming with examples of lines and phrases that are dense in meaning, accurate in psychology, and gloriously speakable. I sometimes wonder whether these few words in *The Tempest* have ever been surpassed in their simple splendour. Miranda has come out of her cave and seen an unexpected crowd of human beings on her father's deserted and enchanted island.

> Oh wonder [she calls out]
> How many goodly creatures are there here!
> How beauteous mankind is! O brave new world
> That has such people in 't.

Here is another quotation from Shakespeare to lead us to the next point. The first scene of *Hamlet* takes place on the battlements of the castle of Elsinore. Some soldiers on guard-duty have been waiting and watching for the Ghost of Hamlet's father who recently died. As twelve o'clock strikes they are relieved by the next sentries. 'Have you had a quiet guard?' one of them asks. The other replies

Not a mouse stirring.

The question is answered. But the words do more. They convey absolute silence. They also bring to our imagination the picture of mice scuffling in an old wainscot such as might have been found in a castle haunted by a Ghost that walked the battlements in the middle of the night. Shakespeare was a master at making the simplest words do many jobs at once.

The famous French writer, André Gide, once made a translation of *Hamlet* which was produced by Jean-Louis Barrault. His version of the line was

Pas un souris qui bouge.

It's an exact translation. But the words 'qui bouge' instead of setting off the imagination to create all kinds of visual images highly relevant to the situation, are a simple statement of fact.

This is not to suggest for one moment that English is a more expressive language than French. Both have their virtues and their defects. Both have words and phrases that are untranslatable. Both have a fine literature. But it is a good example of the kind of disaster that is unavoidable in translation.

Translation, especially of poetry, is never easy. It's far more than turning the words of one language into another. Some years ago I produced *A Midsummer Night's Dream* with a group of students who came from many parts of Europe. We gave a tri-lingual production with the comics speaking English, the lovers German, and the fairies French. The German translation of Schlegel preserved the romanticism of the lovers but lost their wit. The French fairies were wholly unenglish but enchantingly delicate. Puck's lovely lines

Through the forest I have gone
But Athenian found I none
On whose eyes I might approve
This flower's force in stirring love.

became

> En vain j'ai parcouru le bois.
> L'homme m'échappe par ma foi,
> Sur les yeux duquel ma fleurette
> Doit prouver sa vertu secrète.

The French words create a different sort of Puck from the English, sharper, nimbler, more tomboyish, less magical perhaps.

Words, I have said, are the material of the dramatist. They are a large part of the means by which he enables the actors to express their meaning to, and make their impact upon, the audience. It is perhaps for this reason that every play, wherever it was written, from earliest times until the middle of the Elizabethan age, was written in verse. Poetry is both sharper in meaning and richer in emotional impact than prose, and dramatists have usually understood this very clearly. Most languages fall naturally into certain rhythms of speech. The English language, for instance, lapses with devastating ease into iambic pentameters, the form of prosody which was developed to perfection by Shakespeare.

> It's time to stop the game and go to bed
>
> I go to work each day at nine o'clock
>
> The speaker clearly hadn't much to say

One can make up such lines as these with dangerous facility.

The natural shape of French verse is the line with six stresses known as the alexandrine. Recently, in a Metro train in Paris, I wrote down all the notices and advertisements I could see from where I was sitting. Here are some of them.

Tampon YOM-SAVON laine d'acier au savon

Nettoie mieux sans efforts, n'abime pas les mains

Les contrevenants s'exposent a des poursuites correctionelles

These are not lines of which Racine would have been proud but they are tolerable alexandrines, all of them.

Finally, to press home the point, here is a little joke (in very bad taste). The first four lines are from *Phèdre*. The source of the fifth . . . ?

> J'ai revu l'ennemi que j'avais eloigné,
> Ma blessure trop vive aussitôt a saigné.
> Ce n'est, plus une ardeur dans mes veines cachée :
> C'est Vénus tout entière a sa proie attachés,
> Le train ne peut partir que les portes fermés. . .

These examples will show how languages fall into certain natural rhythms. It's therefore evident that translation, which is a very desirable practice, destroys something which is native to the original work and which it is very difficult adequately to replace. An alexandrine, so close to the spirit of French speech, simply cannot be written in English, nor an iambic pentameter in French.

Even if we insist that the translation of poetic texts should be undertaken only by genuine poets, we would probably find that the more successful the translation in its own language, the less true it would be to its original. Which is to say that the perfect translation of a poetic drama is something we can expect to find as rarely as a four-leafed clover. Fortunately many of the European classics are in prose which does not give rise to anything like such difficulties.

We see these problems very clearly when we come to consider translation of the ancient Greek dramatists. Let me take as an example a single passage from Aeschylus's *Epta epi Thebas* (*Seven against Thebes*). The play describes the outcome of a quarrel between Eteokles and Poluneikes, the sons of Oedipus. Eteokles rules Thebes and has banished his brother who at the beginning of the play has led an army against the city. Poluneikes and six other generals lead the attack on the city's seven gates. Eteokles appoints six generals from his own side and determines to defend the seventh gate himself even though this means opposing his own brother. Battle is joined. The brothers kill each other. The funeral procession is described by the chorus in a passage of long attenuated lines that mark the slow forward march of the funeral. Then the brothers' two sisters appear in mourning, crying out their lamentations in short sonorous phrases quite miraculously charged with meaning. (The passage is not only deeply moving and highly effective dramatically, but shows the remarkable internal inflections of Greek verbs.)

The two women, Antigone and Ismene, speak alternately.

> paistheis epaisas.
>   su d'ethanes kataktanon
> dori d'ekanes
> dori d'ethanes
> meleoponos
> meleopathes
> ito goos
> ito dakru
> prokeisai
> kataktas
>   ee
>   ee
> mainetai gooisi fren
> entos de kardia stenei
> io io pandurte su
> su d'aute kai panathlie
> pros filou g'efthiso
> kai filon ektanes
> dipla legein
> dipla d'oran
> achthea tonde tad' enguthen
> pelas adelphe adelpheon

We will now see how this passage fares in a couple of standard translations.

> Smitten thou didst smite.
> > In dying thou didst slay.
> With spear thou slewest.
> > With spear passedst away.
> Sad guest,
> > Sad fate
> > Was thine who liest low.
> Groans—
> > Tears—
> > > For thee,
> > > For thee who gavest the blow.
> My vext soul raves—
> > My heart doth inly mourn—
> For thee
> For thee
> Once Thebes's pride—
> > To misery born.
> Killed by thine own.
> > Destined thine own to quell.
> A twofold sorrow—
> > To behold—
> > > To tell.—
> The burden of our grief is drawing near.
> Brother to sisters. Brother, I am here.
>
> > [Translated by Lewis Campbell
> > in the World's Classics.]

And here's the second.

> Smitten, thou didst smite.
> And slaying, thou wast slain.
> By the spear thou didst slay—
> By the spear thou wast slain—
> Unhappy in thy deed.

Unhappy in thy sufferings.
Let lament be poured forth.
Let tears be poured forth.
Thou liest prostrate—
Thou who didst slay.
Ah me!
Ah me!
My mind is maddened with wailing.
And my heart within me moaneth.
Alas, alas, thou all-lamentable.
And thou also all-wretched.
By thine own thou wast slain.
And thine own thou didst slay.
Twofold to relate—
Twofold to behold—
Are these sorrows anigh unto those—
Anigh, kindred unto kindred.

> [Translated by Herbert Smyth in the
> Loeb edition of Aeschylus.]

Is either passage a successful piece of translation, clear, speakable, an adequate rendering of the original? Hardly; but the difficulties are clearly prodigious.

Translators have therefore tended to do one of two kinds of translation, either a literal version which gives a more or less word for word rendering of the original without seeking literary distinction, or a much freer version which has come to be called an 'adaptation'. Unfortunately the commercial theatre of today tends to take advantage of this situation and in cutting all the plays it presents exactly to suit, as the managers believe, the tastes of the audiences for whom they cater, they require their translators to adapt in a care-free and, as I sometimes think, a quite irresponsible manner. In his most interesting book *The French Theatre Today* Harold Hobson quotes an example of how Jean Anouilh's play *Colombe* was almost completely rewritten for the London stage. Of course the copyright laws ensure that this freedom is not used without the permission of the author but it is well to remember that when we are criticising a dramatist whose work we know entirely through translation, we may be missing some crucial quality of the author's literary style or discussing a rendering of which he may be completely ignorant.

Even in the titles of French plays English managers and translators have assumed a good deal of independence. Who would imagine that *Tiger at the Gates* was the English title of Giraudoux's lovely play *La Guerre de Troie n'aura pas lieu* (The Trojan war will not take place), or that *Duel of Angels* is English for *Pour Lucrèce?*

On the other hand many plays have become more celebrated in adaptation than in their original. Plautus and Terence plagiarised consistently from Greek dramatists whose names, apart from Menander, are hardly known to us. Shakespeare and Molière, in turn, borrowed liberally from Plautus and Terence. Molière's *L'Avare* is far better known than Plautus's *Aulularius* and Shakespeare's *Comedy of Errors* than *Menaechmi*.

I wonder what Shakespeare, looking down from the Elysian Fields, has thought of recent adaptations of his own plays. Did he recognise *The Taming of the Shrew* in *Kiss Me Kate?* or *Romeo and Juliet* in *West Side Story?* And as for Bernard Shaw—*Pygmalion* never had the success of *My Fair Lady*.

BOOKS FOR FURTHER READING:

For a survey and a summary of the world's dramatists there is Allardyce Nicoll's encyclopaedic *World Theatre*, an indispensable work of reference though marred by many singular and very individual judgments. There is also the American John Gassner's far-reaching *Masters of the Drama*.

I should like to be able to recommend some good books on language but it appears that philologists who can expatiate on the history, meaning, and science of words, are not always able to use them in a very interesting manner. For an amusing and stimulating survey of English as well as many foreign languages I recommend *The Loom of Language* by Frederick Bodmer. An admirably readable book which fully expresses my own interest in the link that unites language to culture is Harold Goad's *Language in History*.

For reasons that will already be evident I have made the first mention of every play in its original title so that you will be able to discover, for example, that Griboyedov's *Woe from Wit* and *The Importance of Being Clever* are both translations of the same play, *Gove ot uma*.

I wish that for the same reason publishers would risk a touch of pedantry by always printing the original title of the play on the title-page of a translation.

CHAPTER TWO

The Tragic Drama of the Greeks:
Aeschylus, Sophokles, and Euripides

DRAMATIC art, the art of writing and acting plays, was created in Athens roughly, and as far as we can tell, between the years 540 and 490 B.C. Prior to this date there had been a great deal of both ritual drama and dramatic ritual in countries such as Egypt and India, but nowhere did these rituals develop into drama as in Greece.

The world's first plays are usually referred to as Greek drama or Greek tragedy. The word 'Greek' is misleading. The Greeks have always called their country Hellas and themselves Hellenes. Greece and Greeks are anglicisations of the name the Romans gave to Greece when they conquered it and made it a Roman province. But 'hellenistic' is the adjective applied by scholars to Greek culture when in Roman times it was disseminated throughout the Mediterranean. And then again the only Greek people who went in for writing plays were the Athenians so that the most accurate term would be Athenian tragedy. And that's the subject of this chapter.

Athens in the sixth and fifth centuries B.C. was a city-state, about the size of an English county, extremely jealous of her own culture, and often engaged in bitter warfare with other city-states such as Corinth and Sparta. It's important to understand how this came about.

Greeks of the fifth century were composed roughly of four

different groups. First of all there were the original inhabitants of the peninsula who were generally known as 'Pelasgians' which means 'people of the sea'. Round about 2000 B.C. the peninsula was invaded by tribes of warriors from the north who swept over the country, established their capital at Mycene in the Peloponnese and came to be called Achaeans. These are the people whose exploits are celebrated in the Homeric poems. Around the year 1100 the country was again invaded this time by people called Dorians who settled largely to the west of the Peloponnese and are thought to have been the people responsible for the destruction of the Minoan civilization on the island of Crete.

These various invaders established cities which owing to the mountainous nature of the country had very poor communications with each other and so became jealous of their independence. Cities therefore became city-states.

Athens was probably settled neither by the Pelasgians, the Achaeans, nor the Dorians, but by people who came from the Asiatic mainland to the east. In the sixth century Athens and her neighbouring cities were part of a loose confederation known as Ionia which included the Aegean islands and the Greek cities on the coastline of Asia Minor.

By this date the mixed inhabitants of Greece, infected by the same contagious air, had caught something of the spirit of pan-hellenism. The achievements for which classical Greece has become famous were wrought not only by the Athenians but also by the people of Corinth, who were Dorians, and of many another celebrated city. Indeed, until the time of Perikles it is doubtful whether a visitor to Greece would have considered the achievement of the Athenians in any way superior to what he had seen in many other city-states.

The Greek name for these states was 'polis' (hence politician). They were usually ruled by a tyrant who was sometimes an oppressive monster, sometimes a liberal dictator, who ruled, as Perikles did Athens, with the support of a

democratic constitution. The rather loosely organised democracy of Athens, in some respects one of the city's most
brilliant achievements, represented a kind of compromise that
had been developed in the course of the sixth century when
the three classic political groups, nobility, merchants, and
people. had struggled for a place in the sun. Each political
group that had contributed to the wealth of the city
demanded to be represented in its government. The result was
that under the three most successful politicians of the century,
Solon, Kleisthenes, and Peisistratos, the Athenians achieved a
memorable compromise.

The tyrant with which we are most concerned was Peisistratos. After several unsuccessful though highly imaginative
attempts to win power, he finally became tyrant in 560. He
governed a city of about three hundred thousand inhabitants of
whom nearly half were slaves. It was a splendidly sited city,
dominated by a rocky plateau on which was situated the
Akropolis, or city centre, close to a fine harbour, and surrounded by several thousand acres of arable soil enclosed by
mountains.

Peisistratos faced a political situation which was made increasingly complex by certain religious difficulties. Greek
religion is not easy to understand. The intellectual genius of
the people went into philosophy : they had no gift for
theology like the Jews. Broadly speaking there were two
religious traditions in Greece. Firstly there was the ancient
religion of the Pelasgians, a religion of cults and rituals
devoted to placating the dead and ensuring the fertility of the
soil; and then there was a more recent religion which had
been introduced by the Achaeans, a religion that has become
celebrated for the extraordinary richness of its mythology.
Indeed, so widely popularised have been the often scandalous
exploits of the gods and goddesses whom the Greeks thought
inhabited the cloud-capped summit of Mount Olympus that
we are apt to forget that the myths enshrine in popular form

the most ancient attempts at preserving historical facts—before the Greeks themselves had developed the art of writing history—and explaining natural phenomena.

The problem facing Peisistratos was to find a way of reconciling the religions of the two hostile social groups—the upper and lower classes. His solution was to support them both. He flattered the upper classes with their respect for the Olympians by initiating an extravagant building programme of temples and shrines. He arranged for the Homeric poems to be carefully edited by the knowledgeable and able Ionian rhapsodists, for it was in these poems that the exploits of the immortals and the heroic exploits of the ancient Greeks were memorably recounted. He found little difficulty in encouraging the cults of the peasantry for these were widely observed in all their crude and unsavoury ritual; but he was faced with a considerable problem in the growing popularity of a god called Dionysos who had won a wide following among the workers and peasantry. Dionysos was the son of Zeus and Semele by whom he had a miraculous and painful birth; but he was never accepted by the astocracy as a genuine Olympian and this was embarrassing to Peisistratos.

Both forms of Greek religion involved a good deal of ritual which had as its purpose the fertility of the crops, protection from ghosts or some similarly practical outcome. They were therefore celebrated at the appropriate time of the year in the form of a religious festival. These festivals became the opportunity for pan-hellenic celebrations when men from many different city-states met together and took part in all manner of contests, mostly, though not exclusively, athletic. The origin of these contests has been traced back to the ancient rituals of the Pelasgians and Achaeans when tribal leaders were chosen in personal combat. Contests of many different kinds played a continuing role in Greek life.

In addition to the pan-hellenic festivals there were many local celebrations in each city-state. In the course of the Attic year there were about twenty festivals, each of them lasting several days: the Diasia to appease Zeus; the Anthesteria in honour of Dionysos; the Thargelia, a festival of purification; the great women's festival known as the Thesmophoria— Aristophanes wrote a comedy about it; and every autumn the Eleusinian Mysteries, a feast of purification and fertility before the autumn sowing. The incomparably vivid myths of Demeter, Persephone, and Orpheus form the 'book' of these Mysteries.

Peisistratos had important political reasons for cultivating the worship of the god Dionysos in spite of the fact that as god of the vine the most wild and hysterical outbursts of ecstasy were perpetrated in his honour. Dionysos was also celebrated chorally with a hymn that was known as a dithyramb, a curious word of obscure derivation. In earlier times the dithyramb appears to have been improvised, which, if the celebrants were intoxicated, is not surprising. But in the course of the sixth century the worship of Dionysos began to take a more recognisable artistic form. Dithyrambs were sung in Sikyon; while in the neighbouring city of Corinth they were composed by a certain poet-composer called Arion, about whom some amusing legends have been told. Unfortunately none of Arion's dithyrambs has survived and we do not know whether they actually celebrated Dionysos by name and in person. But we do know that in honour of the god he wrote what he called 'tragic choruses' and that these were performed in some way in a circle.

Nothing is more contentious than the exact meaning of the word 'tragic' and 'tragedy' as it was used by Arion and his successors, but it seems almost certainly to have had something to do with the goat which was given as a prize in the competition—for even the singing of dithyrambs was competitive—and with singing. It's important to remember that it had nothing to do with misfortune or calamity. That meaning was applied to it as a result of the distinctive nature of the plays which the Athenian dramatists called 'tragedies'.

Peisistratos showed his support for Dionysos by establishing in Athens yet another festival, particularly appropriate to the god, and with brilliant judgment gave it the form which he rightly thought would win the support of every social class.

The City Dionysia was a competitive drama festival. On the first of its five days the statue of Dionysos was brought from its temple in the city and born at the head of an exuberant and gaily dressed procession to Eleusis, a village on the frontier of Attica where it had originally belonged. Then after hymn singing and the sacrificial slaughter of bulls—an example of how the elegance and sophistication of Greek culture has its reverse in the most primitive and barbaric rites —the statue was carried back to Athens and placed in the middle of the circular dancing-floor (the orchestra) in the theatre (which simply meant a seeing-place) on the south-east side of the Akropolis.

On the second, third, and fourth days of the festival, plays were given competitively and on the fifth day there was a contest between the Athenian tribes in singing dithyrambs.

This spring-time festival was of supreme importance in the Athenian year, celebrated as a public holiday, supported by the Athenian notabilities who, together with as many people as could crowd into the theatre, stood and sat round the circular dancing-floor and ranged themselves up the sides of the Akropolis on the wooden benches which had been provided. (The celebrated and impressive stone theatre is of a much later date.)

Now we have the setting for the drama: how did plays come to be written?

Scholars argue that when Aristotle stated in his book *Peri Poetikes* (*Concerning Poetry*), for some curious reason always referred to as *The Poetics*, that 'tragedy grew out of the leader of the dithyramb' he did not know what he was talking about, for to us there is no definite connection between dithyrambs

—a choral choreographic performance—and tragedy, a dramatic one.

Yet I think we shall be continually frustrated if we hope to be able to follow every step. The Athenians were a highly inventive and resourceful people and it's clear that where music, poetry, and dancing were involved they were quick to improvise and skilful in finding their way to new achievements. We must also remember that in those days there was no clear distinction between those three arts. Poetry, music, and dancing had little independent existence.

It is generally agreed that the person chiefly responsible for the creation of tragedy was a certain Thespis. He won a victory in the dramatic contest in the year 534 which suggests that contests were already taking place by this date. He is generally thought to have written 'tragedies' for chorus—would we knew how they differed from dithyrambs—and then to have introduced a single actor which he played himself. (The collusion between Thespis and Arion is obvious.) There is no evidence that these tragedies had any connection with Dionysos and some scholars argue that in their early form they were anything but tragic in the modern sense.

We know the names of three dramatists who followed Thespis, Phrynikos, Pratinas, and Choerilos and their plays, to judge by surviving titles, were on contemporary and mythological subjects. Everything tends to suggest that the pre-Aeschylean drama had little of the grave intellectual passion that Aeschylus brought to it. And that brings us to the great old man himself.

The proper name of Aeschylus was Aischulos but it became romanized like many another Greek proper name. He was born in 525 into the nobility. His father was closely associated with the celebration of the Mysteries of Eleusis and, while we do not know whether Aeschylus as a boy was ever a student-priest, we can see in this the origins of his interest in the mythical sources of Greek religion. He wrote ninety plays of which the titles of seventy and the manuscripts of seven have survived. He won thirteen victories in the tragic contests showing that of his ninety plays fifty-two won first award. He was a distinguished Athenian citizen and fought with distinction at the battles of Marathon, Artemisium—a naval engagement—and Plataea. He took a leading part in the production of his plays, introduced a second actor, developed the use of masks, reduced the size of the chorus, and made various experiments with scenery.

He drew the material for his plays, as did the other dramatists, from the mythology enshrined in the Homeric epics, all of which, with the exception of the *Iliad* and the *Odyssey*, have been lost. This is extremely important: for it will be remembered that a little before the time of Aeschylus, Peisistratos had arranged for a definitive version of the poems to be prepared and to be given an honoured position in Athenian education. This was just as if the Bible were in a fragmentary condition and the government had arranged for a collated and carefully edited version to be prepared by the leading scholars of the day; and then ensured that it was given a prominent part in contemporary education. So Aeschylus took for the subject of his plays stories that were extremely well known to almost every member of the great audiences who watched them. When a dramatist knows that his audience is familiar with his story he is able to concentrate on an individual interpretation of the events.

This is exactly what Aeschylus did. The Greek myths are not only enchanting stories but also allegories of historical events and records of interpretations. Now Aeschylus by nature was not so much a story-teller as a poet and a philosopher. In the deepest sense of the word he was a lover of wisdom, a man who was accustomed to wrestle with his material in order to arrive at the truth which lay behind it. No play ever written gives a greater impression of an author doing furious battle with the most profound human problems than *Prometheus Bound* which tells of the conflict between Prometheus, the man who stole fire from heaven and gave it to mankind, and Zeus the father of the gods. Here is no ready acceptance of the benign lordship of Zeus but a fierce and bitter denunciation of the tyrannical behaviour and intolerance of the lord of Olympus. Indeed Aeschylus rarely misses an opportunity to challenge the authority of Zeus and question his integrity. His first play *Iketides* (*The Suppliant Women* or *Maidens*) contains in the long opening chorus a vigorous challenge to the nature and validity of Zeus; for he was in fact challenging the whole of that aspect of Greek religion which was represented by the father of the gods.

For us the most celebrated of his plays is unquestionably the great trilogy on the House of Agamemnon, the most famous of the Achaean kings whose grave has now been laid bare in Mykene together with the very golden treasures which Homer describes. Aeschylus not only tells a gripping story of murder and retribution but argues out the whole moral problem of revenge, bringing one of the greatest issues of the ancient world into open court in the Athens of his own day, with the goddess Athene, the infinitely wise patronness of the city, sitting in judgment upon the issue.

A little perseverance will allow most readers to come to grips with the subject matter of these enthralling plays, especially if they have the chance to see them on the stage; but their form continues to present great difficulties especially to producers. The early plays like *The Suppliant Women* and *Persians* must really be described as works for chorus and soloists, with the chorus playing the bigger part. So the first thing to be decided in staging a Greek tragedy is exactly this —how to handle the chorus; and until this is satisfactorily answered it is useless to attempt the production. Tradition and all too inadequate records tell us that the choral passages were accompanied on the flute; that they were not only sung but danced as well, with a very exact harmony between the measure of the verse—the feet—and the feet of the dancers. For in not so very long a time the tragic chorus of Aeschylus had descended from the tragic choruses in Sikyon, Arion's dithyrambs in Corinth, and the plays of Thespis in Attica, performances which all seem to have had some kind of connection with Dionysos, together with all the choreographic abandon that was associated with worship of the god of the vine. That's to say the chorus of a Greek tragedy in those ancient times, far from being the embarrassed and self-effacing group of actors whom the producer didn't know what to do with that we see today, was the very core, pith, and backbone of the play, ritualistic, orgiastic, swift in movement and clear of voice.

In another respect Athenian dramatists were fortunate; for both music and declamation played a large part in Athenian education, enabling them to play upon a deep and widespread appreciation of the sung and spoken word. The wonderful speeches reported in Thukidides leave no doubt of this. The Greek language is amongst the most flexible and sonorous instruments of speech that have been devised and Aeschylus used it to the full, broadly, with passionate outbursts of sound, subtly, by using the rich internal inflections in the language to wring three or four shades of meaning from a single phrase. It was as well that his audiences could take his stories for granted and concentrate upon the manner in which he unfolded them and the interpretation he put upon them. Greek actors were known for the resonance and clarity of their voices.

The dramatic contests were so arranged that on each of the three days four plays by the same dramatists were given, three tragedies and a satyr play. The latter was an extraordinary genre which requires study on its own. It's enough to say that they were pieces of satirical buffoonery, rather like the frivolous after-pieces in the Victorian theatre, intended to remind the audience, as it appears, of the venal and orgiastic origins of the drama. Whatever their rational explanation it's curious to think that a play like the *Oresteia* was followed in performance by a farce depicting, perhaps, Herakles, roaring drunk and unable even to take one of his own great labours seriously.

It's perhaps even more curious that Aeschylus is reported to have been supremely gifted in the composition of satyr plays. It's the greatest possible misfortune that not a single one of them has survived.

Sophokles (496-406) wrote over a hundred plays, winning eighteen victories and seven second awards. He was never third. As a young man he was celebrated for his personal beauty and for his skill as a dancer. Like Aeschylus he introduced a number of innovations, increasing the number of actors from two to three, and the size of the chorus from twelve, to which Aeschylus had reduced it, to fifteen. He also made improvements in the use of scenery, another subject on which we have only the scantiest information. He too held public office on a number of occasions and wrote what is in many ways the finest of his plays, *Oedipus at Colonnus*, when he was nearly ninety.

Sophokles drew his material from the same historical and mythological sources as Aeschylus but he handled it in a very different way. Critics of Sophokles rightly comment upon the quality of compassion and serenity pervading his plays. In the most tormented, the great tragic masterpiece of *Oedipus Tyrannus*, (variously translated as *King Oedipus*, *Oedipus the Tyrant*, and so on) Sophokles never puts his characters in the position of challenging the appalling destiny that has been preordained for the unhappy king. He never makes war upon an outmoded concept of Zeus as Aeschylus did. He was neither rebel nor reformer but a supremely gifted artist whose creative passions were aroused by the sight of a human being caught up in a chain of disastrous events from which, apparently, there was no escape. To see readily the difference between the two dramatists one may compare Aeschylus's *Choephoroi* (*Libation-bearers*) with Sophokles's *Elektra*, plays depicting the same situation. Where Aeschylus shows Orestes and Elektra protesting at the responsibility for murdering their mother which has been thrust upon them, the Elektra of Sophokles is a pathetic woman, accepting the necessity for avenging the death of her father, but unable and unwilling to question it.

The grandeur of the two plays on Oedipus is rarely questioned. Another of the plays of Sophokles to have drawn considerable attention in recent years is *Antigone* for the subject of the loyalty and obedience a citizen owes his state has been made tragically relevant by the political tyrannies of the twentieth century. (The tyrant Kreon continually makes use of the typically Fascist metaphor of 'the ship of state'.) This wonderful play continues the story of *Seven against Thebes* with which it can very profitably be compared. The general consensus of critical opinion is that Aeschylus is the great hurler of thunderbolts but that Sophokles demonstrates the finest examples of human nobility.

Euripides (484-406) was almost a contemporary of Sophokles, but his style and technique are those of a later generation. With his ninety-two plays presented in something over twenty festivals he won only five victories, a far less distinguished record then that of his predecessors. Indeed, the manner in which his plays were satirised by the comic dramatist Aristophanes confirms the fact that they were by no means popular with Athenian audiences. Many tales tell of the misanthropy of Euripides. He was a recluse and played no part in the life of the city. He was criticised for criticising.

After his death, however, his popularity increased and in time he became the most celebrated of the three. This probably accounts for the fact that no fewer than nineteen of his plays survive.

There is a tendency to disparage Euripides in the light of

his predecessors but this can be misleading. The plain fact is that his plays are the 'easiest' of the three dramatists, more colourful to read and easier to stage; but this is not to say they are better. There are no plays mentioned in this book I would recommend for immediate reading more whole-heartedly than the masterpieces of Euripides, *Troades* (*The Trojan Women*), *The Bacchae*, and *Medea* among the tragedies and *Alkestis*, *Iphigenia in Tauris* and *Helen* among the tragi-comedies.

Once again, by reading the play in which Euripides has handled the story of Elektra (in a play of the same name), we have a splendid opportunity to make a direct comparison of the methods of the three dramatists. Euripides has no truck with the grim fastnesses of the castle at Mykene but sets his play in a rich and romantic countryside. His handling of *Orestes* makes an even more striking contrast with the *Eumenides*. Where the old dramatist develops a classic discussion on divine justice Euripides dramatises the human drama of the situation. Orestes is mad and being nursed by his sister Elektra. There arrive at the palace Agamemnon's brother Menelaus together with his wife Helen, whose infidelity had caused the whole protracted disaster of the Trojan war. As if this wasn't enough Euripides then introduces Tyndareus, the father of Clytemnestra whom Orestes has recently slain in revenge for her having murdered his father, and her husband Agamemnon. A tremendous situation!

It was the very qualities that attracted subsequent generations of audiences that incensed his own. Although he drew his material from the same mythological sources he had no interest in the great cosmic drama that storms through Aeschylus. He had no sympathy for the blind acceptance of destiny that marks the heroes of Sophokles. He was what we should call a realist. His plays responded to swift new trends in Athenian philosophy and to the horrifying developments of the war of Athens and her allies against Sparta and the cities of the Peloponnese. If it wasn't for the perfect artistry of Sophokles I think that today we should respond more readily to the ironies, the fierce cries of protest, and the sheer disgust of human nature that we find in Euripides. Aeschylus is the remotest of the three and the most difficult.

Behind every Athenian tragedy hovers the god Dionysos. To Athenian audiences his existence was revealed as much through the form, the colour, the music, the choreography of the performance, subjects of which we know next to nothing, as through the text itself. His altar was in the middle of, his priests around the edge of the orchestra, the circular dancing-floor. And when the people streamed home after a spring day in the Mediterranean sun, with five or six hours of dramatic poetry singing through their mind, they must really have felt intoxicated, as though they had been filled with the god. Is there a greater reward that dramatic art can give?

I shall leave the Athenian drama with the celebrated scene of the opening of *Agamemnon*. The watchman is on the roof of the palace at Argos watching for the beacons that will herald the return of the king. The lines are transcribed in Greek to remind you that the language is as lovely to look at as it is expressive to hear and to speak.

> Θεους μεν αἰτω τωνδ' ἀπαλλαγην πονων
> φρουρας ἐτειας μηκος ἠν κοιμωμενος
> στεγαις Ἀτρειδων ἀγκαθευ κυνος δικην
> ἀστρων κατοιδα ναυκτερων ὁμηγυριν
> και τους φεροντας χειμα και θερος βροτοις
> λαμπρους δυναστας ἐμπρεποντας αἰθερει.

SOME BOOKS FOR FURTHER READING:

There are many conflicting views about the origin of Athenian tragedy and comedy. It's a fascinating subject though one that need not be studied for an appreciation of the plays.

The first book to be read on this subject might be Sir James Frazer's great classic of anthropology, *The Golden Bough*. For those who find the eight volumes of the complete work a little forbidding, there is an admirable shortened version in one volume.

A different point of view has been argued with great force by Professor William Ridgeway in *The Origin of Tragedy* and *The Dramas and Dramatic Dances of Non-European Races*. They are interesting and important books but rather spoilt by the author's hostility towards anyone with a contrary point of view to his own.

Sir James Frazer's theories are splendidly developed by Miss Jane Harrison in *Themis*, a most readable and important book which contains enthralling chapters by Gilbert Murray on the ritual forms that have been preserved in Greek tragedy and by Frances Cornford on the origin of the Olympic Games. Other short but important books are Jane Harrison's *Ancient Art and Ritual* and Ivor Brown's *The First Player*, a slender book to include among these heavy-weights but an admirable summary of the different points of view.

All the current theories have been critically examined by A. W. Pickard-Cambridge in *Dithyramb Tragedy and Comedy* and all rejected. As a full statement of the sources—for which it is necessary to know Greek—the book is admirable. But I become increasingly convinced, not with Professor Pickard-Cambridge, that while the sources support none of the theories, all the theories have a good deal of validity. The development of Greek tragedy was seemingly both an extremely complicated and very simple process. It was complicated because many elements played their part, ancestor worship, religious ritual, agricultural rites, as well as many more besides those that have been mentioned in the text. But they were used by artists who drew haphazardly, opportunistically from here, there, and everywhere to achieve their purpose. They didn't record their sources. Often they aren't even aware of them.

Nor does art, least of all dramatic art, always develop logically stage by stage. It will stagnate for fifty years and then leap ahead in front of all in one production.

The standard survey of the physical conditions of the Athenian theatre is still A. E. Haigh's *The Attic Theatre*.

The most stimulating survey of the background to Greek tragedy is undoubtedly George Thomson's *Aeschylus and Athens*.

There are innumerable books on the three tragic dramatists but I would particularly recommend J. T. Sheppard's *Greek Tragedy* and Gilbert Murray's *Euripides and his Age*.

On the development of Greek literature I particularly recommend Gilbert Murray's *The Rise of the Greek Epic*.

On Greek religion I recommend Gilbert Murray's *Five Stages of Greek Religion*.

As to translations, for reasons set out in the first chapter, it will be realised that perfect translations do not exist, but there are many to choose from. Gilbert Murray's versions are out of favour. The complete plays of Aeschylus by G. M. Cookson and Sophokles by Sir George Young in the Everyman library are much superior to the translations in the World's Classics. The Everyman Euripides is very poor. A number of the plays appear in Penguin editions. These translations are usually clear and intelligible though lacking poetic quality. The best thing is to choose—or better still, make your own.

There are many admirable books about ancient Greece, but anything written by Sir Richard Livingstone, Rex Warner, H. D. F. Kitto, or H. J. Rose can be strongly recommended.

It is the limited scope of a book of this size that explains the omission of the unquestionable master of comedy, Aristophanes. Comedy grew in a different way to tragedy and the story is an even more uncertain one. But Aristophanes was an Athenian of the fifth century, a contemporary of Sophokles and Euripides, who like the masters of tragedy, found a humble form for his genius and left it an enduring monument of human culture.

Recent translations of some of Aristophanes's plays at least make clear that he was an exquisite poet, a dramatist of tremendous comic invention, a swingeing satirist who found the tragedies of his contemporaries fair game for his ridicule. There have been other poets, other satirists: the unique quality of Aristophanes lies in his inventiveness, his fantasy. In some respects *The Birds* is perhaps the greatest comic masterpiece of all time although *Lysistrata* is more frequently revived.

The satire, and often the whole point of a play by Aristophanes is often so local and contemporary as to be lost on us unless we know a certain amount of Athenian history and literature. They are often very dirty. They are also exceedingly difficult to perform. But the combination of political satire and poetic inventiveness is one from which the drama of the twentieth century could benefit enormously.

CHAPTER THREE

The Comic Drama of the Romans: Plautus and Terence

THE Romans defy assessment. We still live in a Roman world. For every ten words derived from the Greek, there are sixty from Latin. The laws of Western Europe are based on Roman laws, her roads are Roman roads, many of her cities Roman cities. Yet the Romans were neither so attractive, original, thoughtful or individual a people as the Greeks. They hadn't a poet to equal Homer or a dramatist to touch those of whom I wrote in the last chapter. They were plagiarists and imitators of genius, transforming what they gathered into authentic Roman coinage and scattering the Western world with epitaphs of their civilization.

The history of Rome begins properly in the year 510 when her people ejected the last of the Etruscan kings, the famous Tarquinius Superbus. The city consisted of a few thousand people occupying a well situated site on a group of low hills on the south bank of the river Tiber about ten miles from the estuary. Aeschylus was then a young student of fifteen.

To the north of Rome lived the dour and powerful Etruscans. Far to the south the brilliant Greeks inhabited the colonies they had long since founded around the coasts of southern Italy. Sicily was a large Greek island. On every side of Rome there were hostile tribes. In the year 510 Rome, a far smaller city than Athens, was faced with the necessity for prodigies of valour to survive at all. It is hardly surprising that she was backward in creating an individual culture. For three hundred years the Romans fought to establish their political independence, years during which the spirit of those who founded the Republic was thoroughly tested. After bitter wars with Latins, Apulians, Campanians, Sabines, Etruscans, Samnites, and marauding Gauls from the north, by the middle of the third century B.C. the Romans triumphantly could call themselves supreme in Italy.

During these three hundred years the Romans established a tradition of martial valour and administrative skill necessary for success in war. Yet although they lacked a certain quality of originality and creative genius they were a people of discerning taste and substantial achievement. Having numbered the Greeks among the people they had conquered they proceeded to absorb Greek culture with the greatest energy, and in due course the Greek genius and above all the Greek language played as large a part in Roman society as French genius and the French language has done during recent periods of European history. There came a time when the Roman intelligentsia spoke to each other in Greek, wrote letters in Greek. When Julius Caesar was murdered in the Capitol he did not cry out in Shakespearian fashion 'Et tu, Brute!' but 'Kai su, teknon!' (you too, my child).

Plautus was not only the first outstanding Roman dramatist but the first writer of distinction in Roman literary history. He lived the early part of his life in the years when for the first time the Republic had achieved a measure of domestic stability. The emergence of a first-rate dramatist suggests that there was a theatre for which he could write. But what kind of theatres existed in Rome, or even in Italy, in the second half of the third century B.C. is very difficult to say.

Greek religion, as we have seen, was a rather practical affair. The Greeks were a great deal more interested in philosophy than in theology. Roman religion was even more to the point. The Romans had nothing comparable to the elaborate mythology of the Achaeans or the tribal system of the Athenians. For centuries they were concerned with physical survival to the exclusion of all else. When in the year 240 they introduced dramatic performances into their festivals, they were largely copying the Greeks. Although the occasion of the festival was in some respect religious, the plays and the games or contests were wholly secular in nature.

The festivals which included plays were known as the Ludi Scaenici—to be translated perhaps 'dramatic games'. What they celebrated we do not know. But 'ludus' was also a school so either Roman games were more serious than ours or their schools more frivolous. However the Ludi Romani, held in mid-September, were in honour of Jupiter, while the Ludi Capitolini, established in 387 B.C. celebrated the departure of the Kelts after their occupation of Rome.

Meanwhile the Athenian drama had become wholly dissociated from any kind of religious significance and in fact was being exported throughout the Mediterranean world by touring companies of Greek actors who played with increasing frequency in theatres which the Romans were building throughout their Empire. The first plays to be given at Ludi Scaenici were translations from the Greek by a Roman playwright-poet named Livius Andronicus. It is thought that in 240, when a single day was devoted to plays, two comedies and two tragedies were given. But as the drama gained favour, largely the result of the work of Plautus, the number of performances increased until by 214 about four days of the Ludi Romani were devoted to plays and by 190 seven or eight.

The known facts about the life of Titus Maccius Plautus are few and insubstantial. He was born at Sarsina in Umbria in 254. He engaged in some kind of trade, lost his savings, got a job working in a mill and began to write plays in his leisure. He died about 184, aged sixty-nine.

Shortly after his death one-hundred-and-thirty plays were

ascribed to him but scholars think it more likely that he wrote somewhere about thirty. At all events, twenty-one survive.

It is sometimes said, on the most dubious authority, that in his youth he got a job in a theatre—holding the horses of the nobility, perhaps, as Shakespeare is said to have done. I am at a loss to understand this suggestion for there was hardly any theatre in which he could have got a job. Of theatre buildings there must have been one temporary wooden affair in Rome where Ludi Scaenici were celebrated, and there may have been others, even more elaborate ones, in the Greek cities in the South. He may have been a member of one of the small touring companies which played short farces arranged for an established set of characters from one of which he drew his middle name, Maccius. But it would be wholly misleading to imagine that 'he worked in the theatre' in any modern sense of the phrase.

Even so his plays derive quite clearly from two traditions which were very much in opposition. One was the Greek. There can be little doubt that he must have seen performances of Greek comedies given by touring companies in the bigger cities. Culture, at this time, was far and away the biggest export of Greece. These comedies would have been very largely the work of a celebrated poet called Menander of whose enormous output of plays only scraps unhappily remain. But these scraps are enough to show us the changes that had taken place in the Athenian drama since the time of Euripides and his witty contemporary Aristophanes. Gone were even the vestigial remains of religious impulse and ritualistic forms, gone was the trenchant satire and an imagination that could people the orchestra with birds and frogs and wasps, together with one of the wittiest and most musical pens that have ever concocted a comedy; and in place of an Aristophanic splendour there was an urbane and polished comedy, as we might say today, 'of Athenian manners'. It was a comic drama composed of far-fetched coincidences, mistaken identities, love-out-of-season and the course of true love running anything but smooth.

I have said that Plautus drew upon two traditions. One was the Greek. The other was the apparently widespread performances of fabulae or short plays of a humorous, bawdy or rustic kind. Their essential features were that they were improvised (anyway in the time of Plautus) and that they were based on a group of four coarse Rabelaisian characters. To develop this theme properly is the task of the theatre historian. But Plautus may very well have adapted Menander's polished sophistications to his own rough bawdry as a result of the existence of a primitive and undeveloped form of drama on which he was able to build.

Unfortunately not a single one of the Greek plays from which Plautus and Terence drew their comedies has survived so that we have very little idea how much 'adaptation' was involved. But it is clear that Plautus was highly successful in thoroughly Romanising his Greek originals; and if his plays were really as popular as they seem to have been it was because they delighted the Romans and not because they were accurate transcripts of Greek masterpieces.

Yet they were fresh, they were Roman, and a wonderful relief from war; and it's quite evident that the Roman populace turned to these Plautine comedies enthusiastically.

It's not at all difficult to understand the popularity of Plautus. His plays are genuinely funny. Of that there is no doubt. Not to read perhaps, but certainly in performance. They are funny even when played in Latin. It also happens that they are extremely well written in the most stylish poetry. Thirdly, and unless we are very much mistaken, when they were first performed they must have struck Roman audiences as being extremely original. No such substantial, fresh, and thoroughly Roman plays had yet been seen and they had all the stylish polish of the much admired Greeks.

For reasons that have nothing to do with the intrinsic quality of his plays Plautus has turned out to be one of the most influential dramatists who has ever lived—and in this we must couple Terence. The comedies of these two dramatists have been adapted by such writers as Shakespeare and Molière. Yet good translations are rare. Indeed, few notable translators have thought the plays worth their trouble, though successful adaptations have occasionally been made. The problem Plautus sets is that of finding a language that will combine the bawdy zest of the original with a poetic distinction of style. Anyone sufficiently familiar with Latin to read Plautus in the original, even with a crib, will quickly come to appreciate his charm, his humanity, his good spirits, his love of ridiculous situations and sheer good humour which take hold of you and seem to condone the stupidity of the plots, the falsity of the teeming coincidences, the dullness of the stock characters, and the repetitive situations.

Plautus is an excellent example of the dramatist who can only be fully appreciated in the theatre where his varied metres fall unmistakably upon the ear, underlining the situations, emphasising the movement of the action, giving the play that fundamental lyric and choreographic quality which is almost wholly absent from the theatre of the twentieth century.

That the plays of Plautus were successful seems to be indicated by the growing number of days devoted to Ludi Scaenici and the performance of plays. Companies were formed to produce the works of Plautus and the writers who began to imitate him, and a Collegium Poetarium was formed. But unless posterity has been uncommonly hard on the manuscripts and the reputations of the dramatists, there was no worthy successor to Plautus until Terence, Publius Terentius Afer (195-159).

Terence was what we should call today a 'coloured' person. He was of Libyan stock and came from Carthage. As a youth he was purchased as a slave and brought to Rome by the Senator Terentius Lucanus who gave him his name and in due course set him free. Terence is thought to have been physically attractive and extremely intelligent and his master gave him a good education. Indeed the senator seems to have been ready enough to show off the wit of his young protégé and introduced him to a group of distinguished writers associated with Scipio Africanus Minor, who, ironically, was shortly to put an end to the independence of Carthage. And when the young man, then aged nineteen, turned up with a witty adaptation from the Greek, they sent him along to the official who chose the plays for public performance who in turn sent him to a certain well-known old dramatist named Caecilius of whom we do not know very much and of whose little we do know we don't think very much. Terence arrived, so the story goes, when the old man was just about to begin his dinner, and was bidden to read a few lines. Caecilius recognised at once that here was no fumbler, made him sit down, share his meal, and then finish reading his play.

And that's just about all we know of Terence.

The source of much of that scanty information is to be found in his Prologues. He expresses his gratitude to his actor-manager-producer Ambivius Turpio. He defends himself against the accusations of plagiarism by asserting that he is the first to acknowledge his debt to his Greek originals and that if his plays have met with any success it has been due to the skill of the actors rather than the merits of the text. He attributes the failure of one of his plays to the counter-attractions of a rope-dancer and a gladiatorial spectacle. And he hints more than once that the attacks made upon him by an elder dramatist have been prompted by jealousy; and while admitting that he has been accused of receiving benefit from the help of men of rank and station he points out that it is surely an honour to be the recipient of such patronage.

The plays of Plautus suggest their author to have been a

man not unlike our own Ben Jonson, big and bluff, coarse-featured and deep-voiced, with a rolling laugh and a roving eye and, in sharp distinction to all that, possessed of the acutest possible sense of literary style. Terence, on the other hand, we imagine to have been slightly built, with dark complexion and sharp features, a certain elegance of manner and a ready wit. Such portraits may be far from the truth but they suggest the differences in the two authors. Terence handles his themes more delicately than Plautus, his poetry is more epigrammatic, his attitude more sophisticated.

These differences are usually explained by the nature of the audiences for whom they wrote. Terence's audiences were more cultured than Plautus's and contained fewer of the less well-educated. As we say today, they were not so 'popular'. This in turn suggests what is amply proposed by the nature of the plays, namely, that Plautus wrote for a large ebullient audience that paid so little attention to the play that he had to begin by telling the story of what they were going to see and hear and then extending every situation, as it arose, to the utmost; whereas Terence wrote for a smaller and more sophisticated audience of which his master and sponsors were typical. He could thus begin his plays with a Prologue in which he could discuss the kind of professional criticisms which have already been mentioned.

Critical works on Terence make much of his skill in epigrams, citing the famous

> Homo sum : humani nil a me alienum puto
> (I am a man : nothing of man is alien from me)

But what a lot there is to be admired in the simple candour that comes out in a passage like this from the Prologue to *Heauton Timorumenos* (*The Self-tormenter*)—

> adeste aequo animo date potestatem mihi

statariam agere ut liceat per silentium
ne semper servos currens, iratus senex
edax parasitus, sycophanta autem impudens,
avarus leno adsidue agendi sint mihi
clamore summo cum labore maximo.

which may be rendered literally :

Come now with an unbiassed mind and give me authority
to present a comedy that may be followed in silence. There
will be no servant on the run, angry old man, greedy parasite,
fawning ruffian, avaricious procurer, continuously presented
at the top of my voice and with great effort. . . .

BOOKS FOR FURTHER READING :

Two excellent introductions to Roman social history have
been published as Pelican Books—R. H. Barrow's *The Romans*
and F. R. Cowell's *Cicero and the Roman Republic* but they
almost wholly ignore the drama. Justice is done by Edith
Hamilton in her excellent *The Roman Way*.

The general lack of interest both scholarly and popular in
the Roman comic dramatists and the Roman theatre in general
is evident in the paucity of literature about them. The standard
background is Margarete Bieber's *The History of the Greek
and Roman Theatre*. William Beare's more recent study *The
Roman Stage* is scholarly but does not send one racing to the
library to get hold of the texts.

One dramatist alone represents Roman interest in the tragic
drama—Seneca. He wrote ten tragedies on Greek subjects.
Their heavy turgid style represents all that we most detest in
the classical drama. But they played an enormously important
(and baleful) part in the drama of the Renaissance, a subject
that will be discussed in Chapter Six and it is astonishing that
so little scholarly attention should have been given to con-

temporary performances of the single Roman contribution to tragic drama. Seneca was also philosopher, author, and politician of considerable distinction, who brought an element of sanity to the court of Nero and committed suicide on the order of the Emperor.

The theatrical crudity of the plays of Seneca is extraordinary in view of the sophistication of contemporary Roman society. But this perhaps is yet further proof of the manner in which the Romans let the drama die in front of them. They copied Greek architecture and created some magnificent buildings themselves. They copied Greek drama and killed it for themselves and many hundreds of generations after them.

CHAPTER FOUR

The French Dramatists of the Middle Ages: Mercadé, Gréban and Michel

H OW EASY it is to romanticise the life of medieval Europe!
When we look at medieval illustrations, the pictures of
neat little walled towns glowing in new white stone in front
of deep blue skies, with trimly ploughed fields in the fore-
ground; when we look at the stylishness of the clothes that
people wore, the splendour of their architecture, the serenity
of their literature, it's easy to imagine that here was a Golden
Age instead of a period which probably had more than its
human share of dirt, poverty, disease, cruelty and oppression.

Medieval life could not have been comfortable, but it had the
advantage of being more unified than ours. This is important in
considering drama. Medieval people lived under the shadow of
castle, abbey, or city-wall. These were the three great powers
of the Middle Ages—the Baron, the Abbot, the Merchant. To
one or the other of them the people owed their allegiance;
but in defence against them they formed their own allegi-
ances. They knew nothing about their world and little about
their country—as yet unblighted with the curse of nationalism
—but they knew a very great deal about their own community—very much more than the village gossip of the
twentieth century, and this for the very good reason that they
did not peer from behind lace curtains but continually took
part in an active communal life.

There was a time in the Dark Ages when European life was almost at a standstill. There was no trade, no industry; no towns, few villages. In the three hundred years following the first millennium the face of Europe was transformed. Cities were built, industries established, trade increased, there was activity of every kind on every side. And since man is a political animal, the people concerned in all this making, the masters and their men, together with the merchants who bought and sold the produce, formed themselves into Trade Guilds and Unions, not only providing for the organisation of their Craft, but assuming positive social responsibilities towards their members, educating the young, and watching over the welfare of the older members.

The influence of the Church in all this was enormous and not easy to define; for the Church held actual possession of a large amount of European soil and claimed possession of the souls of the people who lived upon it. At the same time the Church Fathers could allow themselves no moment of relaxation in their unremitting fight against paganism. They held the souls of the people in thrall by a hairsbreadth, they could afford to miss not a single opportunity to enforce the Christian message. So we find that the shape of the medieval church and its decoration is dense with symbolism and didactic art. We find that the services themselves, the Church Liturgy, are for the most part a re-enactment of historical events that took place in Israel so many hundred years previously. It is explicitly stated in the Preface to the Catholic Daily Missal that 'the altar becomes each day before the eyes of the congregation a corner of Palestine where there is celebrated with Jesus the events of his life'. A famous Church Father, St. John Chrysostom, who was no lover of the drama, said, 'The celebration of Mass has the same value as the death of Jesus upon the cross.'

But the Churchmen did not confine their impressive and splendid ritual to set hours within the church: they missed no chance to move processionally through the streets of town and village, even of the countryside, displaying their magnificent vestments, singing their fine anthems and doing much to kill drabness and boredom, which are surely things of the devil, with colour and beauty which are of God.

The very fact that Church services were a kind of re-enactment of historic events gives them an essentially dramatic quality. In the course of time certain monks, who in the serene retirement of their lives had opportunity to meditate upon these things, developed a way of enforcing the strength of certain events in the Church's calendar by developing the ritual into a recognisably dramatic form. This led to the growth throughout Europe of what is now called the liturgical drama : plays that were given in the middle or at the end of a service, sung in Latin by the priests, and seeking to make the greatest possible impression upon a congregation which was now becoming an audience. Since the scope of these plays developed till they came very near to disrupting the orderly celebration of the canonical offices, it is not surprising to find that many of the bishops rose in their wrath against them.

We have records of the prohibition of these plays from the twelfth century onwards, but the greatest number come from the thirteenth and fourteenth centuries. By this time the Church was not alone in its encouragement of the drama. In France at any rate there was a fairly vigorous secular drama going on outside the churches, and instigated, for the most part, by a group of men who rarely receive their due in theatrical or literary history. These are the jongleurs, or minstrels.

Such people must not be thought of as street-corner entertainers or throaty ballad-singers. Many of them were poets, composers, and singers of considerable ability. It was almost certainly the jongleurs who composed and sang the superb Chanson de Roland and the other magnificent Chansons de Geste. Taillefer, a Norman jongleur, had led the Norman troops into battle at Hastings singing at the top of his voice.

Poets like Jean Bodel and the highly gifted Adam le Bossu had written enchanting little plays as early as the twelve-seventies. So that when the Church showed an inclination to wash its hands of the drama, there were men in the market-place ready to give it parentage.

One of the most striking works of the jongleurs had been the composition of the story of the life of Jesus in poetic form. This work was known as the *Passion des Jongleurs* and had been composed in the late twelfth or early thirteenth century. So when in the course of time there arose the opportunity to act plays in the open air and on an increasingly ambitious scale, the *Passion des Jongleurs* became one of the sources from which the dramatists drew their material. In those days there was no such crime as plagiarism. Composition was largely anonymous and the sincerest compliment that one poet could pay another was to filch a large amount of his work, reshape it and develop it. This was the usual custom.

One of the ways by which we learn what went on in the Middle Ages is by records of Prohibitions. In days before newspapers there was no need to record what people did; only what they were forbidden to do. So when we find that in 1402 Charles VI granted the right of playing Mysteries exclusively to a religious confraternity called the Confrèrie de la Passion we can be fairly sure that a good many other groups had been accustomed to give performances of Mysteries and not always of a very good standard.

By this time the jongleurs seem to have become something of a spent force. They were not the power they had been in former times; and although the Church had been unforgiving towards the performance of plays in front of the altar, those of the clergy who were interested in literature and drama were given every encouragement to deploy their talents elsewhere.

Thus we come to the period of the great French Mysteries

of the Passion; 'mysteries' because they revealed the mysteries of the Christian religion, and Passions because their climax was the central revelation of Christianity, the crucifixion and resurrection of Jesus Christ. So from the jongleur's Passion in epic form we come to the first great Passions in dramatic form, though whether the earliest, the *Passion d'Autun*, the *Passion du Palatinus* and the very beautiful *Passion de Sémur* named from the place where they were performed or the manuscript was discovered—whether these lovely plays were written by monks or jongleurs or monks turned jongleurs, we have no idea.

The three great Passions which are the subject of this chapter were all written in the fifteenth century and, since each writer began by developing the work of his predecessor, it's not surprising to find that they all follow very much the same pattern in their construction and the selection and treatment of their material. Beginning with the creation of the world and the fall of Lucifer, they show in a vivid form the fall of man together with prophecies of his redemption, the birth of Jesus, his ministry, passion, crucifixion, and resurrection. Within this substantial framework the authors develop, explain, and elaborate the canonical story with the help of a powerful scene for which they found justification in the eighty-sixth Psalm. We are shown how after the fall of man, the figures of Pity, Truth, Justice and Peace turn to God the Father and beseech him to redeem mankind. Their arguments, though a little tedious dramatically, provide a most interesting explanation of medieval theology, as well as explaining God's decision to send his Son down to earth.

The first of these three great Passions is the work of Eustache Mercadé. He was an official in the Abbey of Corbie, a small town near Amiens, where for many years there had been a Benedictine Abbey school. He then became Dean of the Faculty of Ecclesiastical Law in the University of Paris and achieved some reputation as a poet and a theologian.

This stern preoccupation with theology and law is evident in his work which has little of the witty profanities which are to be found, for instance, in the *Passion de Sémur*. Wherever possible he introduces little sermons, homilies, and exhortations to drive home the meaning of the scene. But his Passion extends to 25,000 lines, and although one should not be impressed by size for its own sake, it is a work of enormous power and impressive splendour.

If it had not been almost immediately followed by a work of even greater quality I would dwell longer on this stern and somewhat compelling masterpiece. But Mercadé did little that Arnoul Gréban didn't do a great deal better, and whilst honouring the pioneer we must give our attention to the better poet.

Arnoul Gréban was born in Le Mans around the year 1420. He came to Paris in his teens and took his university degree to become Master of Arts not later than 1444, when he was in his early twenties. He found employment in the cathedral of Notre Dame, where, being a musician, he became organist and choirmaster, a position of some distinction for a young man. He went on to study theology under a certain Thomas de Courcelles, a canon of Notre Dame, an intimate friend of Pierre Cauchon who had conducted the trial of Joan of Arc. In 1451 he became Maître des enfants, or head of the choir school, and so responsible for the education and welfare of about a dozen choirboys.

Now although there are slight discrepancies in all these dates it seems fairly clear that he wrote his *Mystère de la Passion* between taking his degree in 1444, and 1452. We know he had finished it by this latter date since in this year he was visited by a certain Guillaume de Bonoeuil who requested him in the name of the citizens of Abbeville, to accept ten golden crowns for a copy of his work.

Engaged on a prodigious literary and musical composition that goes to 35,000 lines it is not surprising to hear that he found his duties in superintending the choirboys somewhat exasperating; that he asked for permission to have his own key of the library (a request that was granted provided he paid for it himself), and for certain hours of the day reserved for his own activities.

So we can piece together a picture of this gifted young man in the late twenties and early thirties, arguing theology with his master, slipping into the library whenever he could escape his many other duties to compose the text and music of what proved to be one of the masterpieces of medieval art.

I think, however, that it was more than theology that he discussed with his master, for Thomas de Courcelles came from Amiens where he was a notable rhetorician, and Amiens is close to Arras where there had been a celebrated Guild of Jongleurs since 1109, and to Abbeville whose citizens had been quick to request a copy of the masterpiece. It's probable that the towns in the north-east of France where there was a lively tradition in dramatic literature and production, by then had developed a close relationship with Paris where the most brilliant writers and composers were almost bound to gravitate.

Although in a note attached to the beginning of one of the manuscripts of the work Gréban says that he wrote the play at the suggestion of some friends to show that the sins of man may be redeemed by God but not those of the devil, there is no evidence that his friends were members of the Confrèrie de la Passion. At all events it was performed with great success three times in Paris before 1473 and over a hundred times elsewhere. Remembering that the whole work takes four days to perform—it is divided into days instead of acts—and requires two hundred and twenty performers as well as a huge number of scenes, these figures are remarkable.

Of the subsequent life of Gréban little is known for certain. Around the year 1455 he seems to have left Paris and returned to his home town of Le Mans where he became a canon of the cathedral. Here he was joined by his brother Simon and together it is thought they worked on the *Mystery of the Acts of the Apostles*, a cycle of about forty plays in 62,000 lines! Arnoul died in 1471 and his brother survived him by a couple of years.

As to the enormous length of Gréban's *Passion*, the first thing to be said is quite simply that he had no interest in economy. Being accustomed to plays that concentrate the greatest possible intensity of emotion into the shortest possible time, it is all too easy for us to dismiss long stretches of the *Passion* as boring. But the first thing to do is to accept the timelessness of the whole conception. Where the profoundest secrets of our existence are concerned—and to people of the Middle Ages the Passion dealt with nothing less—there is no question of having to finish by a certain time. To hurry an argument or a scene would be a form of blasphemy.

Nor does he attempt to make it easy listening or watching by the introduction of humorous scenes and worldly-wise characters such as the English medieval dramatists loved to write. Herod, the termagant of the English Passions, is hardly characterised at all; the shepherds are the most delightful pastoral figures, and even the blasphemies of the guards of Jesus when he is brought before Herod and Pilate do not destroy the atmosphere of piety that invests the work. Indeed the most typical scene of the whole *Passion* is perhaps that in which Gréban shows us the anguish of Mary when she thinks she has lost her boy in Jerusalem at the time when he is in the temple disputing with the elders. Indeed one can really say that Mary is the protagonist of the work. It is clearly she who most interests the artist in Gréban. His loveliest verse is provoked by her lamentations at the foot of the cross and it is the lightness and gentility and serenity of her character, so gloriously realised time after time in medieval art, that suffuses the whole enormous work with a kind of serene glow.

The whole work has a kind of grave fervour about it, an unforced depth of feeling that continually raises it to the sublime. Most of the verse is the common octosyllabic measure which Gréban varies for different groups of characters. Here for example are the lovely lines with which Gabriel salutes Mary at the beginning of the Annunciation :

> O chère maitresse,
> O haute princesse,
> Dame souveraine,
> par ta grande humblesse
> s'esjoye et esdresse
> notre court hautaine.
>   Car espoir nous maine
> que nature humaine
> par toi se redresses
> à la gloire pleine,
> dont coulpe villaine
> lui tolt sa noblesse.

And here is the lament of the devils when they hear that the redeemer of mankind is about to be born.

> La dure mort eternelle
> C'est la chanson des damnées;
> Bien nous tient a sa cordelle
> La dure morte eternelle;
> Nous l'avons desservi telle,
> Et à lui sommes donnés;
> La dure morte éternelle
> C'est la chanson des damnées.

Then we come to the shepherds whose names are Aloris, Ysambert, and Pellion; we meet them singing one of the many lovely rondeaux with which the work is embellished and for which of course Gréban composed the music himself.

> Est-il liesse plus series
> Que de regarder ces beaux champs
> Et ces doux agnelets paissants
> Sautants en la belle prairie.

I hope that even if you are unfamiliar with French you will have attempted to speak those lovely passages over to yourself. One can't help feeling that the critics who complain of the stilted quality of the verse must have very insensitive ears. Here are a few lines of the measure with which, in verses of thirteen lines with a complex rhyming scheme, Gréban introduces the three kings.

> Je te salue, Dieu du ciel glorieux,
> Dieu immortel, Dieu sur tous vertueux,
> Vrai fils de Dieu, qui creas ciel et terre;
> Je te salue, roi par dessus les cieux,
> Monarque seul du monde et tous les lieux
> Que coeur humain peut penser ni enquerre. . .

The researches of the great scholar Gustave Cohen have yielded us a fairly clear idea of how a Passion of this kind was staged. Each individual scene had its little stage or 'mansion' set side by side along two or three sides of a market-place or 'place' or against the north wall of a cathedral. This kind of simultaneous setting gives Gréban considerable scope in the arrangement of his scenes, enabling him to 'cut' from one to another without any of the problems we meet in the Elizabethan theatre where a quick succession of short scenes tends to be scrappy. This is particularly effective in the Passion sequence where around the central figure of Jesus he can show us God's compassion for the agony of his Son, the laments of Mary, the anthems of the angels, the hysterical cries of the devils, the hostility of the Jews, the indifference of Herod and Pilate, the blasphemies of the centurions, and the despair of the disciples. Professor Cohen's researches have made clear that no pains were spared to increase the realism of the stage effects so that the earthquake at the death of Jesus would have been stage-managed with considerable ingenuity and effectiveness. I wonder whether these performances at their best were not among the most notable theatrical productions that have ever been staged.

I say 'at their best' because it wasn't long after the death of Gréban that decadence set in. In the latter part of the century the custom of writing *Passions* proliferated. Their already enormous scope was extended by Jean Michel, a doctor of Angers who was required by the citizens of Angers, a town on the Loire, to write the biggest and finest Mystery that had yet been staged. He obliged by taking Gréban's text and secularising it. This enormous work of 45,000 lines was staged at Angers 'sumptuously and triumphantly' as the manuscript tells us, in the year 1486.

There is no doubt that by using every possible means to secularise the Bible story, turning many of the characters into figures of contemporary France, replacing the piety of Gréban's text with a fierce and realistic realism, he did much to advance the cause of dramatic art. But he helped to destroy Christian art. It was in fact the very exuberance and worldliness of so called Christian dramatists, composers, sculptors, and painters that laid the Church open to criticisms of idolatry from without and irreverence from within.

Besides, it was at this very time that the art and ideas of the Italian Renaissance were becoming widely know in France. In 1494 Charles VIII had made an abortive invasion of Italy and the returning armies had brought back tales of fantastic artistic achievements. Against the cold cool ideas of antiquity, the sprawling blowsy Mysteries, the very antithesis of the ideals that were being propounded by he humanists, began to appear intolerably vulgar. They were not even substantiated by profound religious convictions. In 1548 the Parlement of Paris forbade the Confrèrie de la Passion to stage the *Mystery of the Passion of Our Lord* and other sacred Mysteries in the city. The brotherhood gave performances in Normandy. In 1556 the town council of Rouen made a similar prohibition. They went to Bordeaux. The same thing happened. The medieval drama was at an end.

Meanwhile the Catholic Church had already begun to reform itself from within. For a number of years its leading bishops had been sitting in council in Trent. Thereafter there were Christian dramatists. But there has never again been a Christian drama.

Meanwhile in 1552 with the production of one of the most uncompromisingly classical pieces that has ever been written, Etienne Jodelle's *Cléopâtre captive* a new chapter in the theatre was opened.

BOOKS FOR FURTHER READING:

Grace Frank's *French Medieval Drama* gives all the facts but it's rather dry to read. An essential companion to this book for anyone who can read French is Gustave Cohen's *Le Théâtre en France au moyen age*. Professor Cohen was a fine scholar and to him we owe much of our knowledge about the manner in which the Mysteries were staged.

There is a chapter about the British dramatists of the Middle Ages, who were almost always anonymous, in my companion book, *Masters of British Drama*.

Joan Evans's *Life in Medieval France* vividly describes the social life of the period and is admirably illustrated. J. Huizinga's *The Waning of the Middle Ages* describes in an enthralling way the essentially dramatic quality of life in the later Middle Ages.

Texts of the French Mysteries are extremely hard to come by, but no one should despise the admirable Larousse edition of *Le Théâtre religieux au moyen age*. It contains excerpts and summaries especially of Gréban's *Passion*. The cost is a couple of shillings.

It is quite extraordinary that complete texts of the works described in this chapter should be virtually unobtainable in France except in the most scholarly libraries. English treatment of her medieval (though anonymous) Mysteries is a little better. The texts of the Early English Text Society are obtainable in most libraries. Full editions of modernised versions of the York and Wakefield plays—both masterpieces of medieval literature—are also available.

CHAPTER FIVE

The Spanish Dramatists of the Golden Age: Lope de Vega and Calderon

T HE DRAMATISTS to be described in this chapter lived during the period that is known as the Golden Age of Spanish drama. The dates are approximately 1580 to 1650. It was the Elizabethan and Jacobean age in England, the beginning of the classical age in France, a period of decay in Italy.

It's curious that there should be little adequate literature about a country which for a time was by far the most powerful and influential in Europe and which has always been a fascinating one. The Spanish Armada, the courtship of Queen Elizabeth by Philip II, the so-called conquest of the Netherlands, and the Spanish Inquisition are a few of the more clearly defined features that stand out from a huge misty canvas of British ignorance about Spain in the sixteenth and seventeenth centuries.

To begin with, then, who were the Spaniards? A people bearing traces of Goth, Kelt, Roman, Arab, Jew; whose mixed ancestry is clearly to be seen in the marvellously varied architecture of her cities; who, if we take the year 1580 as our starting-point, had enjoyed political unity for barely a hundred years.

As a result of her energetic conquests in the New World and a succession of fortuitous (or politically expedient) marriages on the part of her kings in the Old, she had acquired enormous possessions both in Europe and overseas. She had imported gold in considerable quantities and thereby increased the power of the monarchy and the nobility far beyond what was good for them, at the same time and quite incidentally almost wrecking the economy of Europe.

Backed by inflexible minds and enormous wealth the rulers of Spain showed no inclination to reform her culture with humanistic ideas or her Church with non-conformist ones. In a rapidly changing world they not only preserved but actually developed the country's medieval institutions. During the Golden Age, when the Spanish creative genius was struggling to express itself, the Spanish court, with its slow, stately and elaborate ritual, demonstrated the utter inflexibility of temperament that eventually destroyed the country. The common picture of Spanish grandees stalking haughtily across Europe and looking down their long thin noses—marvellously well painted by El Greco—at anyone whose pockets were not lined with gold, is substantiated by the facts.

The literature and drama of the Golden Age give us a vivid picture of powerful and not always very scrupulous noblemen. The dramatists—for all the sycophancy that is evident in their attitude to the king—suggest continually that it was the nobility who were the oppressors, the kings who were the protectors of the poor. But a rather patronising attitude to the peasantry was about as far as they got in recognising the cause of the eventual impoverishment of the country. For the Spanish peasants were not only oppressed, they were ignored by successive governments. In the exquisite cities of Burgos, Valladolid, Seville, and Granada, a traveller would have met as lively a people as any in Europe; but in the countryside he would have recognised symptoms of the malaise that was to destroy the place of Spain among the powers. Much of the country's soil was poor, the rainfall was sparse, but the cavalier indifference of the nobility towards the people was worse than anything.

Yet it must not be thought that Spain was a dismal country to live in or that her people were unable to laugh. The mixture of races has produced a verve and a gaiety which generations of bigoted monarchs have been unable to destroy. Even today Spaniards are among the most lively and stylish dancers in Europe.

And so in the sixteenth century the Spanish drama grew because its roots were in the rich dramatic tradition that had been cultivated as in so many other European countries during the Middle Ages. Plenty of fascinating secular plays were written. But the most remarkable plays were religious. Far from banning the Mysteries the Spaniards wrote bigger and better Mysteries and called them *Autos sacramentales*. At a time when Europe was alight with the ideas that are known as the Renaissance they set up the most rigid barriers against European thought. It's true that in the Autos there are traces of humanism but that is a matter of literary criticism. Compared with Italy, France or England, Spain was almost wholly unaffected by one of the great intellectual upheavals in the history of man. Humanism, of which more will be said in the next chapter, made far less impact in Spain than it did elsewhere. Church and monarchy closed the doors of the establishments of learning to what were really heretical and pagan studies. So in Spain there was no great classical revival which produced plays like Etienne Jodelle's *Cléopâtre captive*—and a host of Italian imitations from the Latin which did irreparable harm to the European drama and destroyed the Italian almost until the present century.

The development of the Spanish drama was thus due only in small measure to the humanist ideas of the Italian Renaissance. It owed more to the ancient tradition of religious drama, and to the natural lyrical genius of the Spanish people whose actors used to break out, even in the middle of the most solemn religious Autos, into an exciting and licentious dance that was deplored by the Church as the 'pestiferous zarabanda'.

The history books give a catalogue of the names of the men who in the early part of the sixteenth century began to create a Spanish drama—Juan del Encina (1468-c. 1537), Bartolome de Torres Naharro (c.1480 - c.1530), Gil Vicente (c.1465 - c.1539) and many others, men who for the most part were either connected with a noble household and wrote for private performances, or who were employed by the Church. Yet there is certain evidence that a more popular kind of drama was developing with the emergence of professional companies—for actors do not take up acting as a profession unless there are plays to act and a reasonable expectation of audiences to watch them. We have in fact a description of a performance by a small professional troupe from the pen of no less a person than Miguel de Cervantes, the author of *Don Quixote*. The scene is Valladolid. The director of the troupe and its leading actor was a certain Lope de Rueda, a goldsmith who had given up his trade to 'take to the road'. The stage consisted of six planks laid across four benches in the form of a square. The décor was a blanket. The music was supplied by an unaccompanied singer behind the scenes. Costumes, wigs and properties could have been put into a single sack. But by popularising realistic incident and the vernacular of the people Lope de Rueda, in his simple way, advanced the cause of dramatic art. (Amusing and vivid descriptions of the lives of actors on tour in Spain and France are to be found in a couple of novels of the period, Augustin de Roja's *El viaje entretenido* (*Entertaining Journey*) and Paul Scarron's *Le Roman comique*, later in date (1651) but true to the spirit of the period.)

In 1561 Madrid became the capital of Spain. The managers of the many small companies lobbied the authorities to build them some kind of a theatre. The authorities cleverly evaded their responsibilities by giving the job to the confraternities of charitable citizens such as had existed in most European countries throughout the Middle Ages. The confraternities opened a so-called theatre which in fact was little more than a rough stage set up in the middle of a yard formed by the backs of three houses. Around the stage were benches. The arrangements were primitive and the performances crude— but they became immensely popular and two more confraternities opened theatres. In other Spanish cities, notably Valencia, Seville, Saragossa and Granada the same thing happened. During the sixteenth century the religious canon of the drama lay heavily over Spain and performances were only allowed in the cities on Sundays and Feast days. But such was the popularity of the theatre and the extent of the profits, that the licence was extended to cover Tuesdays and Thursdays. By the end of the century plays were given on one-hundred-and-ninety-eight days of the year; and the Spaniards found themselves in possession of a vigorous, indecent and extremely popular theatrical movement. There was of course no end to the wagging of heads. The Church begged the king for suppression. In 1598 he succumbed. The confraternities petitioned. The king relented and eventually a compromise was reached; but by the sixteen-thirties there are thought to have been several hundred theatrical companies playing throughout the length and breadth of the country; and their existence was made possible almost wholly by the work of Lope de Vega.

If Lope de Vega was truly a man of his time, and we have no reason to suppose that he was not, he is a corrective to the picture of Spain as a land of rather staid and splendid grandees who lived upon Mexican gold and the toil of the poor. He was a man who went with his time, not against it. He had humble parents but at school he was precocious. At fifteen he was a soldier and at sixteen he sailed with the Spanish Armada against Britain. He became a clerk in minor orders but could not accept the discipline of an office job. Though a devoted Catholic he was passionate and erotic and by no means a model Christian. He slandered his enemies, fought duels, accepted banishment when the judgment went against him, was ever on the look-out for sinecures, entered a monastery, carried on a tempestuous love-life and produced an enormous literary output. Apart from a large number of novels and poems it is computed that he wrote somewhere about two thousand plays. Over four hundred exist and the titles of more than seven hundred are known. Yet nobody who loves the man has ever asserted that his claim to fame rests solely upon the extent of his output.

Lope de Vega is a supremely able dramatist, and we must not allow snobbery to weigh against him when we set him beside other masters. He treats a very wide range of themes but he does not approach the universality of Shakespeare. He is no dullard in probing the shifts of human behaviour but he has nothing like the intensity of Racine. He writes of the moral code but not with the splendour of Corneille. Nor has he the profound wit of Molière. He has something of a great many dramatists and yet for all that his own individuality of style. Few dramatists have approached the speed of the action of his plays. His stories are exciting, plausible, swift-moving, original, and often coloured by the bite of his irony. In his treatise on playwriting there occurs the often quoted passage in which he writes of 'locking up the laws of the drama with six keys and banishing Plautus and Terence from his study'. His purpose, he says, is to 'write in a manner that will draw the greatest possible applause from the spectators.' There can be little doubt that he succeeded in his object and it is not surprising that a growing number of theatrical companies looked to him for the bulk of their repertory.

Lope de Vega has been badly served by the translators. This is surprising for his plays present few of the problems that make Plautus and Racine, for example, almost untranslatable; and in view of the similarity of tone that exists between the Spanish and the Elizabethan drama he might well be accorded the popularity in this country that could never be expected for Racine or Corneille. The translations that do exist almost always miss one of the most attractive qualities of his work, the easy racy verse, almost doggerel on occasion, but splendidly speakable and lengthening into sonnet-form when the action slows and the emotion is lyrical. The theatrical virtues of this literary form have been pointed out and fully discussed by Mr. Somerset Maugham in *Don Fernando*. Again we have a similarity between Spain and England. It was enormously easier for a dramatist to write in popular verse form when verse was commonly composed and spoken aloud. Courtiers of Philip II would converse together in sonnet form and an Elizabethan nobleman was expected to be as adept at handling a lyric as his sword.

The Spaniards have a vivid epithet for Lope de Vega. They call him the 'Monstruo de la Naturaleza', which roughly means the 'freak of nature'. For in spite of the exquisite precision of his language there is frequently a kind of unruly and overflowing abandon about the way he handles his themes, and this energetic lawlessness gives an impression of vigorous realism. Although he was a realist who wrote from what he observed and was inspired by what he saw, he dipped his pen deep in romanticism. His women are habitually beautiful, the victims of lustful noblemen, constantly saved by the justice of the king who hands them back to the peasant boy who has loved devotedly since childhood. But even a hackneyed theme like that can be transformed by the quality of the writing. *Macbeth* is at bottom a blood-and-thunder melodrama. Shakespeare continually made magic of novelettish situations, yet no one questions his right to be considered the supreme spokesman of Elizabethan England. So was Lope de Vega of Philipian Spain. Do not let me give the slightest impression that Lope's plays are stupid pieces of romantic nonsense. A few have been translated into English, *El mejor alcade, el rey* (*The King the Greatest Alcalde*, 1635), *Lo cierto por lo audoso (A Certainty for a Doubt,* 1625), and *La estrella de Sevilla (The Star of Seville,* 1615). They contain a rare mixture of poetry, romance, and most perceptive observation. In particular let me recommend a play that has become celebrated in recent years, *Fuenteovejuna,* sometimes called *The Sheep Well* (c. 1625), one that should be familiar to the theatregoing public of every country in the world.

Yes, a talent this which might well have been a Shakespeare or a Molière; but an intelligent artist needs an intelligent public, and while we don't want to dismiss Spanish theatre audiences as idiots it is important to realise that the crowds who surged round the rough open-air stages in the Spanish cities had to be held by the gripping quality of the story, the effectiveness of the theatrical situations; the bite of the language. They were a very different audience from the knowledgeable intellectuals who supported Molière's performances at the Palais Royal; they included only occasionally educated churchmen or members of the nobility who were frequently to be seen in Shakespeare's Globe. A dramatist, even more than other artists, is very much a victim of time and place and the theatrical conditions of the age in which he is writing. A dramatist of outstanding genius can restore the status of the drama just as a group of poor dramatists can forfeit it. But he needs qualities of character which in some respects are outside his skill as a dramatist.

The dramatists of the Golden Age, Lope de Vega, Tirso de Molina (1584-1648), Alarçon, and Calderon lived during the reigns of the two most disastrously incompetent kings in Spanish history; men who under the influence of evil advisers, and a corrupt nobility threw away in fifty years the grandeur that had been won by Charles V and Philip II. But it's dangerous to overplay the interrelationship between drama and society; for against a background of oppression, poverty and corruption, we have to set a robustious popular theatre, a score of fine dramatists, at least two of which were of outstanding ability, a number of fine actors, and actresses of sufficient charm to form alliances with the king himself.

Philip III had played no great part in the cultural life of his country; but his son, Philip IV, with the great protruding lower lip, was a thoroughly lazy fellow without the least interest in government but a passion for the arts. He refused to live in the superb Escurial, one of the most magnificent buildings in the world, where his father had spent most of his life, and had his own splendid palace built in the neighbour-hood of Madrid. Here in the Buen Retiro he created a centre of dilettante society where wits and parasites could circle aimlessly at pleasure. His chaplain, his chamberlain, and his secretary were among the leading writers of the day and he gave his patronage to such artists as Velasquez, Zurburan, Murillo, and Ribero. He and his wife had a passion for the theatre and continually visited the two public theatres in Madrid as well as attending the many private performances that were given in his private theatre in the Buen Retiro.

It is here perhaps that we find the key to the paradox of Spanish society, for it was by his example that people broke loose from the bigoted and straight-laced Catholicism which Philip III had imposed upon the country and behaved with a licence that increased the popularity of the theatre and under-mined its dignity.

Pedro Calderon de la Barca (1600-1681) began his profes-sional life, like his near contemporary Lope, as a soldier. There is nothing surprising in this for the compromising political position of Spain in Europe made it necessary for her to keep an enormous standing army which was a drain upon her physical resources as well as on her population. At the age of twenty-nine he gave up soldiering and took to playwrit-ing. He was clearly possessed by something of the demonic energy that drove Lope de Vega, for in the course of the next fifty years he wrote upwards of two hundred plays.

In 1635 the indolent Philip IV made him manager of the

theatre and of theatrical performances at the Buen Retiro where he spent a large amount of his time. An unhappy love affair turned his attention increasingly towards religion and in 1651 he was ordained a priest. The king, however, forbade him to relinquish his practical interest in drama and pointed out the value of his religious plays to the service of God.

In literary histories Calderon is always referred to as the dramatist of the 'baroque'. This term, which is commonly used in Europe, is little understood in Great Britain because, the situation that gave rise to the baroque not having arisen, we have very few genuine examples of this form of art. Baroque is the art of the Counter-Reformation. Its inspiration was fundamentally Catholic. That is why we find very little baroque in northern Europe where the Reformed Church became established and the Catholic counter-offensive made less headway. Baroque art, and I include sculpture, painting, music, architecture, and drama, begins with the rigid sense of form which Europe had learnt from the Renaissance; but on top of this form there is laid the most elaborate ornamentation and decoration. Calderon is more of a baroque dramatist than Racine, the subject of the next chapter, because although his plays, and specially his Autos, are just as tightly constructed, they are far more florid in language and visual in presentation. It is not easy to judge whether Lope de Vega was a baroque dramatist owing to the scarcity of copies of his religious plays, but his secular dramas are far too romantic and un-classical to come under this heading. Calderon, however, wrote under the eye of the most Catholic king in Christendom. The canons of duty and honour run through his plays like a reiterated dogma. He uses the same short fast moving verse form as Lope though with a good deal less variety. He handles his richly romantic stories with considerable discipline. He subjects his situations to his themes. While as a practical man of the theatre he is always ready to bring off a striking effect, he is not a theatrical opportunist, ready to sacrifice everything for a compelling scene or an impressive situation. He is grander than Lope, deeper in thought, but usually less theatrically exciting. He provokes more thought but less emotion. His characters are less exuberant and compellingly alive but his stories are more closely knit.

His secular plays represent little more than half his work. There is hardly a Spanish dramatist from the fifteenth century onwards who did not try his hand at religious drama. But most regrettably this movement, the interest of which extends far beyond the Catholic content of the plays, has never been properly documented or described. Indeed I have not been able to find a single authentic picture or description of the manner in which these plays were staged during the seventeenth century. This is the more provoking since the little we do know suggests that we have here the most fascinating combination of French Mystery, English Passion, Italian Triumph, and Catholic ritual.

Performances of these *Autos sacramentales* were given on the midsummer Feast of Corpus Christi—the occasion for similar plays in England in the fifteenth century—and on the following day or days. Each city appointed an official with the responsibility of selecting the managers whose companies were to stage the plays, and which plays they should perform. This was all done at least four weeks in advance. On the day of the Feast the professional theatres were closed so that the actors would be free to take part in the Autos. At the height of their popularity in the seventeenth century performances were given not only in the squares from carros or carts, as in England, but in the professional theatres and even within the great cathedrals themselves. Calderon's enormous output of Autos is partially explained by the number of requests he received for Autos from the chapters of the great cathedrals of Madrid, Toledo, Granada, and Seville.

Spanish critics credit Calderon with between seventy and eighty *Autos sacramentales*. Their stories are taken from the old and new testaments, history and legend. They are not of great length, most of them taking, I would judge, an hour-and-a-half to perform. They are heavily didactic in the manner of English morality plays like *Everyman*, but they give tremendous opportunities for spectacular scenic effects and very considerable sums of money were spent on staging them.

In *Los encantos de la culpa* (*The Sorceries of Sin*, c. 1633) Calderon shows us Man and his Five Senses enduring the storms of life aboard a ship at sea. Man is likened to Ulysses, and Sin, who beguiles him with her sorceries, is the counter-part of Circe. (A good example this of the influence of classi-cal mythology.) *El purgatorio de San Patricio* (*The Purgatory of St. Patrick*, 1635), describes the astounding exploits of the saint in Ireland, and *Los dos amantes del cielo* (*The Two Lovers of Heaven*, c. 1636) with its Roman setting has much in common with the theme of *Quo Vadis*.

The cast list of some of the Autos gives a good idea of their allegorical nature. *La cena del rey Baltasar* (*Belshazzar's Feast*, 1634) has the King, Idolatry, Vanity, Daniel, Thought, Death, the statue of a horseman, and some musicians. The famous *El gran teatro del mundo* (*The Great Theatre of the World*, 1645) has the Author, the World, Discretion, Beauty, the Rich man, the Poor man, and so on.

Other Autos, such as *El divino Orfeo* (*The Divine Orpheus*, 1663) and *La vida es sueño*, (*Life is a Dream*, 1677) open with elaborate stage directions which give a magnificent idea of the splendid way in which the elaborately decorated cars came slowly through the streets bearing the most elaborate scenery. These enormous carts, like sumptuous versions of our own rather impoverished Lord Mayor's procession, are still to be seen in Spanish streets at Corpus Christi, but plays have not been acted from them since 1765.

Calderon outlived his master and principal patron, Philip IV by sixteen years. The young king was a child of four when he succeeded his father. The Regent, Marianne of Austria, had little love for the theatre. Calderon had little interest in the publication of his plays during his own lifetime and this makes it extremely difficult to date them. But so far as one can judge he seems to have enjoyed the opportunity to be released from the responsibilities of a court dramatist, to pass the last years of his life as a priest and composer of religious plays. I fancy that his grave beauty and the softly modulated voice of which his contemporaries speak, were better fitted to the quiet of a cloister than the artificial splendours of the Buen Retiro or the Escurial.

BOOKS FOR FURTHER READING:

Spanish dramatists have been poorly served by English biographers. There is nothing more recent on Lope de Vega than Hugo Albert Rennert's *The Life of Lope de Vega* and Calderon does not appear to have been honoured at all.

The Spanish drama of the Golden Age has fared little better. There is Rennert's *The Spanish Stage in the Time of Lope de Vega* and some interesting material in the second volume of George Ticknor's *History of Spanish Literature* published in 1849! But in Somerset Maugham's beautifully written *Don Fernando* the reader will find some vivid pages on Lope, Calderon, Tirso de Molina, and the whole Spanish background.

Translations of Lope de Vega's plays are few and hard to come by. Half-a-dozen are available in an American paper-back edition.

There is a well-known collection of some of Calderon's secular plays in a translation by Edward Fitzgerald. Some of his Autos have been translated but they too are scarce.

Calderon wrote his most famous play, *Life is a Dream*, in two versions, one secular and one as an Auto. They are fascinating to compare.

CHAPTER SIX

The French Classical Dramatists: Corneille, Molière and Racine

T HE THREE DRAMATISTS who are the subject of this chapter wrote a number of plays which are generally accepted as masterpieces but which are notoriously difficult to come to terms with. The English can make little of Corneille and Racine and allow Molière his reputation without ever having deeply appreciated his plays. There is evidence that even the French are tending to find the great classical masters remote from the spirit of the age; and even if they have not replaced Racine with Shakespeare in the Comédie Française, the masters of comedy are enjoying far greater popularity than the tragic dramatists of the seventeenth century.

The difficulty lies not so much in the plays as in the society which they so brilliantly and succinctly crystallised. The customs and behaviour, the ideals and attitudes, the whole social structure of the court of Louis XIV and le Grand Siècle are so remote from the twentieth century that the superbly vital Jean Racine himself and all the courtiers who strutted through the courts and gardens of Versailles, tend to appear like actors in a distant historical pageant.

French classical tragedy was one of the most distinctive and perfect expressions of French humanism. The ugly phrase lies heavily upon the page and yet in many ways the period was one of the most joyous and exuberant in the history of man. In the course of the sixteenth century there were those who thought that man stood upon the threshold of the Golden Age.

People of today may find it difficult to appreciate the enthusiasm with which men and women of the fifteenth and sixteenth centuries discovered the literature and art of antiquity. I understand it very well myself for when I first learnt Greek, some twenty-five years after leaving school, I too experienced this intoxication, and yet the culture of ancient Greece came to me as much less of a revelation than it did to the French and Italian humanists for whom it was a blaze of sunlight falling across the dark and limited land-scapes of medieval thought. The great cry of Pico della Miran-dola, one of the most colourful young scholars of the Italian Renaissance, summed up this sense of pagan enthusiasm when he cried out, 'To man alone is given the possibility of growth and development solely dependant upon his own free will!'

However far back we trace the origins of the movement that we know as the Renaissance, its full impact came at a time when the Christian Church was badly in need of reform. Yet leading churchmen were classical scholars and many an artist was a devoted Christian. There is no separating the strands of Reformation and Renaissance. It was a time of renewed thought, renewed activity throughout Christendom, and the twin movements of ecclesiastical reform and pagan humanism cross-fertilised each other so that it is no longer possible to disentangle cause from effect.

The religious issues were far too profound to be solved by Church councils, university seminars, and government com-missions. The age of Louis XIV with its insistence upon manners, self-respect, and authority, was created in the shadow of the Massacre of St. Bartholomew when French Catholics butchered some three thousand Protestants; and of the Wars of Religion which desolated the French countryside and left a forbidding landscape of towns destroyed, starving peasants, and universal lawlessness.

A few words about the work of three great men, widely different in every respect though they were, may give an indication of how people thought and felt at this important period of French history.

The spirit of humanism is gloriously evoked in the poems of Pierre Ronsard who as a young man in his twenties was a member of the group that included Etienne Jodelle, the author of *Cléopâtre captive*. The success of the play was such that all France, we are told, 'was soon filled with the sound of the author's name'. But in the long run it's Ronsard who has been remembered by posterity for his poems that evoke pictures of blue skies and beautiful women, lawns and gardens and antique statues, all tinged with a kind of languorous paganism and sophisticated bitterness.

The Counter-Reformation of the Catholic Church was initiated by one of the greatest of its leaders, St. Ignatius Loyola, the founder of the powerful and ubiquitous Jesuits. Opening his famous *Spiritual Exercises* almost at random we find him exhorting the Christian reader to worship God through all his faculties of sight, hearing, smell, taste and touch. In contemplating Hell the Christian must 'see with the eye of the imagination those great fires, hear with the ears the lamentations, cries and blasphemies against Christ and his Saints, he must smell the smoke, the brimstone, the refuse, the corruption, he must taste the tears of conscience and feel how those fires do torture and burn souls'.

Scarcely less passionate was the work of a curious Protestant poet, Théodore Agrippa d'Aubigné. In *Les Tragiques*, a mighty, sonorous, hyperbolical, rhetorical, passionate poem, stuffed full of theatrical effects, lush mysticism, sensual imagery, and an intensely erotic conception of man and God, he presents a most forbidding picture of the dangers attending a godless and embattled France.

These three men are examples from the large number of artists and writers of outstanding quality and of that individuality which today we call 'character', who show the many-sidedness of the age and the depth and variety of the passions that stirred it. The efforts of Henry IV, the famous Henry of Navarre, Louis XIII and XIV and their ministers, brought peace to the country, but they did not resolve the tensions that finally exploded in the events of 1789. They did however direct the attention of the middle and upper classes upon the important subject of the quality and nature of civilised living. In their intellectual life, appreciation of the arts, human relationships and the cultivation of such adjuncts to good living as cooking and the manufacture of first-rate wine, the French became the leaders of Europe. The middle and upper classes responded to the political and religious peace and turned their attention to the social reconstruction of their country and of their class.

Outstanding leadership in this laudable ideal was given by a lady, Catherine de Vivonne, Marquise de Rambouillet. This tall, striking and attractive woman was the wife of an official in the French court, but finding life in the royal entourage to be boisterous, crude, and lacking those qualities of refinement she took to be the essentials of civilised living, she used the excuse of the birth of a daughter, Julie, in 1607, to retire from court and establish a literary and artistic salon at her house, the Hôtel Pisani, which was situated in the centre of Paris and which she had inherited from her father. By her charm and intelligence she attracted the leading writers and thinkers of the day and her circle grew in popularity. What was more, people began to take it seriously. The Marquise and her associates set about raising the moral tone and intellectual standards of society in general and literature in particular. Authors, young and old, new and established, read their works and subjected them to criticisms from the company. Discussions were held on the use and pronunciation of words and details of literary style. They did much to give the French language its present enviable qualities of suppleness, clarity and grace.

Their outstanding work was in establishing canons of civilised behaviour. They began that study for which the French have become celebrated, the study of man. They popularised such terms as 'gallantry', the conduct befitting a gentleman, the need for a man or woman to have plenty of 'bon sens' and 'bon esprit'; they tried to create the ideal of a normal civilised man, intelligent but prone to certain weaknesses of a typically human kind. The dramatists presented ideal heroic types in their plays. They also presented both the prodigious passions and the human failings to which even heroes are susceptible.

In the early years of the seventeenth century the French drama had been sustained mainly by the plays of Alexandre Hardy (c. 1576-c. 1631). He wrote over six hundred plays of a romantic kind. He used a great variety of stories and he felt himself bound by no rules in handling them. So he wrote plays in the medieval manner, much shorter than the great Passions, of course, but with rambling stories and continual changes of scene. In Paris they were staged at the Théâtre du Marais on a stage that was cluttered with little pieces of scenery representing the various scenes of the action.

To the humanists, to the denizens of the salons, the scholars and intellectuals of the time, the plays of Hardy and the like were beneath contempt, and wholly lacking in those civilising qualities which they expected to be demonstrated in every kind of art and culture. They drew their authority from Italy, for everything Greek or Roman was canonical. They made earnest study of Aristotle's *Concerning Poetry* and Horace's *Art of Poetry* and composed their own rules for dramatic art. By the sixteen-thirties they had won considerable authority for their views and looked around for a dramatist who might be expected to exemplify them in his work. Their choice fell upon the ineluctable and unfortunate Norman, Pierre Corneille.

Pierre Corneille (1606-1684) was born in Rouen and educated at a Jesuit College which gave him a wide knowledge of classical literature and experience in the production of Latin plays. (Practical dramatic art was a feature of Jesuit education for several hundred years throughout Europe.) When not at college Corneille saw the performances of plays by Alexandre Hardy which were regularly staged in Rouen by a touring company headed by the fine actor Guillaume Montdory. By the time Corneille had reached his twenties Montdory was established in Paris at the Théâtre du Marais and it was therefore to him that Corneille sent his first play, *Mélite*. Between 1630 and 1635 he wrote a number of comedies which had a reasonable success and brought him to the notice of the great Armand du Plessis, Duc de Richelieu, who was interested in the drama and had his own theatre in his palace. In 1635 Richelieu played a part in the formation of the Académie Française. This institution was the creation of nine scholars who intended that it should carry on the work of the salons in establishing standards for French language and literature. Among these nine scholars was a certain Jean Chapdelain who turned his grave and humourless mind to theories of dramatic art and produced the rules that have already been mentioned. Wishing to see these principles realised the Academy invited the young Corneille to write a classical tragedy which should be a model of its kind. Corneille obliged with *Le Cid* which largely owing to its splendid verse and great actability has become a classic of French dramatic literature.

Le Cid was an enormous success with the public; but it was not a satisfactory example of the principles which had been laid down by the Academy. The pundits, infuriated by the play's success, opened a vicious pamphlet war. Corneille replied rather ineffectually, for he was a poet and not a journalist, and while he was not without his supporters, he was severely treated by the professional critics.

There is much that is silly in *Le Cid*, but these stupidities are almost wholly the result of Corneille's unsuccessful attempt to compress the action of the play into twenty-four hours as was demanded by the 'rules'. Its success was due to his immense poetic talent, his flair for developing vivid theatrical situations, and his good sense in choosing a theme, that of family loyalties, which was close to his own heart as well as the interest of the public.

Corneille weathered the storm and after a short rest in Rouen went on to write the group of plays on which his fame securely rests: *Horace* (1640) and *Cinna* (1641), plays dealing with political loyalties, *Polyeucte* (1642), on religious loyalties, *Le Menteur* (1643), the only comedy he wrote during that period of his life and a most enchanting play, and his superb *Nicomède* (1651).

Corneille wrote as a man who had the reconstruction of his country at heart. The problem that interested him was the nature of authority. Where did it lie, a man's loyalty to his family, to his religion, to his state? Where is the supreme authority when there is a conflict of loyalty? They were subjects of profound importance to audiences of the mid-seventeenth century.

In the plays of Corneille we are able to watch how a dramatist with a large, expansive, generous and sympathetic mind finds freedom and grandeur within the rigid disciplines of classical drama. And the outcome of this absolute harmony of expression is to give classical tragedy, at its most perfect, a quality of aesthetic serenity that is not to be found elsewhere in the theatre.

Towards the end of his life Corneille wrote *Examens* or short essays on his plays and included them in the printed editions. It's curious to see him exercising his muscles in support of the Rules, in attempting, it is thought, to keep in line with his young rival Racine. But there was no need for this rather craven gesture. He had his own qualities which the more perceptive of his contemporaries fully realised and which were generously celebrated by La Bruyère in one of his most famous essays.

Between 1652 and 1659 Corneille wrote no more plays; but his work found a champion in the young man who succeeded him as the leading dramatist of the day, Jean Baptiste Poquelin who took the professional name of Molière. (So close in fact was the friendship of the two men that a French scholar has recently advanced the theory that the plays of Molière were actually written by Corneille!)

Molière, like Corneille, was educated at a Jesuit College; similarly receiving a thorough education in classical literature. At the age of twenty-one he was drawn to the theatre, joined a company, and after initial failures, spent the formative years of his life, from 1645 until 1658, touring the provinces with a troupe for whom he acted and wrote plays, and of which, on his eventual return to Paris, he was the leader. He was now thirty-six; an accomplished writer of conventional comedies and considerably influenced by the methods of the Italian companies whom he met continually 'on the road'; a good actor and admirable producer.

Molière opened his first crucial season in Paris with a revival of Corneille's *Nicomède*. This seems to us a curious choice because it invited direct comparison with the actors at the Hôtel de Bourgogne, who, led by the bombastic Montfleury, were celebrated for the excellence of their tragic style. The style of Molière's company was quieter, more naturalistic, and not very much appreciated. He followed *Nicomède* with four more tragedies by Corneille. They all failed.

Molière was always ready to fight for his principles. We know something about what they were from *L'Impromptu de Versailles*, a play about acting which he wrote some years later. This play shows us quite clearly why he disliked the style of the Hôtel de Bourgogne and deliberately invited comparison. Moreover like many artists with a turn for comedy he had deep-rooted ambitions to shine in tragedy, longing to 'ronfler les vers' and 'faire le brou-ha-ha', which means roughly to act in a bombastic and rhetorical manner.

Fortunately he had been accustomed to give his own light-hearted farces as after-pieces. These won great favour with his audiences and enabled him to move to a better theatre, the Petit Bourbon, which he had to share with a company of Italian comedians.

The fibre of the man now becomes evident. Instead of setting out to ingratiate the by-no-means easily pleased Parisian public, he produced a new comedy of his own composition in the form of an acute satire upon the more ridiculous aspects of the salons, a group of people one would have thought a young dramatist would have gone out of his way to please. *Les Précieuses ridicules* set a royal fluttering in Parisian society; and when he followed it with *L'École des femmes*, a more daring play than Parisians were accustomed to laugh at, there were plenty of people to say that the man was a re-incarnation of the devil. My heart warms towards the anonymous voice which at the end of the first performance called out, 'Courage, Molière, violà une bonne comédie!'

But his courage was not in question. He answered the criticisms of *L'École des femmes* with a play entitled *La Critique de l'école des femmes*, which is again of extraordinary interest for the light it throws on his beliefs and ideals.

There were plenty who did recognise his talent. Among his most loyal supporters was the King himself, then a gay young man sixteen years younger than Molière, not yet soured by a sense of mortifying religious guilt, and still determined to make the court of Versailles the centre of a lustrous age. No one was better fitted than Molière to supply him with the entertainments he needed. The musical plays which Molière wrote for performance at Versailles or Fontainebleau are altogether stylish pieces, the most successful and celebrated probably being *Le Bourgeois Gentilhomme*.

Patronage in high places had now secured him a better theatre, the Palais Royal, the former private theatre of Richelieu, of which he remained in possession until his death in 1673. But patronage did not blunt his pen and between 1664 and 1666 he wrote his three masterpieces, *Tartuffe*, *Don Juan*, and *Le Misanthrope*. *Tartuffe* created such a fury among the churchmen that it was suppressed for five years and then performed in a somewhat modified version. *Don Juan* was suppressed after fifteen performances and not printed till after his death. *Le Misanthrope*, the most ferocious of all, created less opposition because the target was more general. Alceste's great outbursts against the treachery, cowardice, self-interest and injustice of society could be dismissed as the ravings of what we should call today 'an angry young man'. But in this superb comedy there is to be found the very heart of Molière's attitude to life and the summit of his protest.

Molière is known to posterity as one of the great comic dramatists of all time. He is honoured in the theatrical profession as a pre-eminent 'homme de théâtre', a phrase for which there is no translation. For there was no aspect of theatrical art in which he did not excel.

He was the manager of his company, and although this is a function that means little to the general public, this work is essential to the success of any theatrical venture. It involves responsibility for policy, advertising, choosing the plays, organising the construction of scenery, supervising the sale of tickets, payment of wages, and innumerable other financial details which can be far more exhausting and far less satisfying than genuine creative work.

In addition to being the manager of his company he was also its producer, as the position is usually called in England, or its director as the Americans say, or stage-manager as it was called until the turn of the twentieth century. The French term 'metteur-en-scène' is the best term of all for it describes exactly what he does. He puts the play on the stage. *L'Impromptu de Versailles* confirms the view that Molière's artistic standards were high and that his company achieved an ensemble unique for those times. The tremendous comédie-ballets which he wrote for performance at one or other of the King's courts must have been particularly arduous to create, especially when he was obliged to collaborate with the brilliant but odious little Italian-born composer, Lully.

Finally he was an actor, a leading member of his own company, playing those rich 'character' parts of which his plays are full. There were those of his contemporaries who found it hard to understand how the author of *Tartuffe* could stoop to play a part like Scapin in his own play, *Les Fourberies de Scapin*, a contemptible rogue of a character who ends up being beaten in a sack. These intellectuals did not understand Molière's understanding of theatrical art. He would simply reply that his presence on the stage was necessary for the sake of the performance and the livelihood of at least sixty other people.

And it was as an actor that Molière died. He became fatally ill during the last act of the fourth performance of his satirical comedy *Le Malade imaginaire* and died an hour or two after the fall of the curtain. He was only fifty-one. He had been ill for some years and his death was not unexpected. But the real cause was not tuberculosis so much as the rivalries and jealousies, the continual slander and malice to which this honest and outspoken man had been subject throughout a large part of his professional life.

Molière lived to see the early successes of the third great dramatist of the century. Jean Racine was born in 1639 near Paris. Intended for the Church he was educated not by the Jesuits but in the Jansenist monastery of Port-Royal. The theological deviations of the Jansenists from what most Catholics were required to believe are irrelevant. Enough that the dispute was a bitter one. But their educational reforms were striking. While subjecting their students to a rigorous classical education as the Jesuits did, they believed that no young man should be taught to write or speak Latin or Greek until he could use his own language, French, with grace, clarity, and style. This aspect of Racine's education must at least partly explain the source of the limpid, melodious but sonorous language of his plays.

1664 was an important year. Molière was at the height of his powers, and Corneille, now a man of fifty-eight, was back in the theatre. Between 1658 and 1674 he wrote eleven tragedies which were all failures and are held in little esteem today. His close and abiding friendship with Molière did not greatly benefit him and in the writing of tragedy he was worsted by the stripling Racine, thirty-three years his junior.

Racine, the son of wealthy parents, brought up by wealthy relatives, provided as a young man with a succession of sinecures, a courtier from the moment of his first introduction to the young king at the age of twenty-four, was born with the proverbial silver spoon in his mouth. He was personable, handsome, a brilliant conversationalist, and immensely attracted by and attractive to women.

Molière, whom he met at court, was responsible for the staging of his first play, *La Thébaïde*, which dealt with the story of Oedipus, and in view of the appreciation with which it was received went on to stage his second, *Alexandre*. But there the friendship between the two men came to an end. Molière's company was unable to compete with the players of the Hôtel de Bourgogne in tragedy and artistic rivalry was soon sharpened by personal jealousies. Molière's beautiful leading lady, Marquise du Parc, moved over to the Hôtel de Bourgogne and Racine sent his plays with her.

This was the beginning of the great creative period of Racine's life. He wrote eleven masterpieces at the rate of almost one a year from *Andromaque* in 1667 until 1676 when

he crowned his dramatic career with the great masterpiece of
Phèdre.

All this time he led a vigorous private life which gave plenty
of opportunities for salacious gossip of which there were
spiteful people in plenty to take advantage. He was bitterly
attacked by his former masters at Port-Royal for becoming
involved in the theatre and for writing highly sensual plays;
but controversy and criticism, far from driving him into semi-
seclusion as they had Corneille, sharpened his pen, and it was
not until the most bitter of all controversies that followed the
production of *Phèdre* that grace seemed to go out of him. He
nearly became a Carthusian monk, changed his mind, married
plump and plain and had seven children. Twelve years after
the production of *Phèdre* he returned to the drama and wrote
two great religious plays, *Esther* (1689) and *Athalie* (1691), at
the instigation of Madame de Maintenant, for production at a
seminary for young ladies of which she was a governor.

Now although I have often been moved by these plays, both
in reading them and in seeing them performed by the company of the Comédie Française, I remember too well the
agonies of boredom I endured in studying *Bérénice* for School
Certificate to dismiss lightly the tremendous difficulties
implicit in them for English audiences and English readers.

First of all the titles that fall dully upon the ears: *Bérénice*,
Andromaque, *Iphigénie*, *Phèdre*. Who were these remote and
forbidding creatures? The answer is that they are the most
tempestuously passionate women who have ever been created;
whom the author has stripped of glamour, of self-control, of
every worldly consideration and revealed in all their stark
misery. Racine reveals an aspect of the human heart that
Shakespeare never drew. Cleopatra is not devoured by a con-
suming passion for her Anthony anything like as intense as
that of Phèdre for her son-in-law, Hippolyte, or Andromaque
for her dead Hector.

Then we are put off by the dull musty dustiness of the

classical theatre. This results from a failure to perceive the astonishing skill with which Racine masters the extreme limitations and disciplines of the form he has imposed upon himself, the tightly-wrought construction of the plays, the tight form of the verse, the simple undeviating development of the story without a line or an incident introduced to pad, divert, or elaborate. In a play like *Phèdre* Racine seems to drive a scalpel straight to the deep-lying centre of a woman's anguish and reveal starkly the emotions that are throbbing there. Even if we do not enjoy a play of this kind, it is not difficult to admire its technical perfection.

They may be perfect, but they are dull. Yes, they are remote from the twentieth century and written in a manner that is not readily acceptable to English audiences. Moreover they do not easily surmount inadequate performances. But anyone who has seen Edwige Feuillère in *Phèdre*, or Marie Bell in *Bérénice*, or Gérard Philippe in *Le Cid* will begin to realise their immense vitality and the effect of this emotional concentration. These legendary, mythical, and historical characters become prototypes of human behaviour. No one has ever loved so desperately as Phèdre, or faced such intense political decisions as Horace, or acted so resolutely as Polyeucte.

So we'll make an attempt to appreciate the perfect construction of these plays, the quality of their verse, the intensity of their emotion, but can anything forgive the interminable length of the speeches? Can a play be intensely dramatic when the characters seem to speak in monologues? The answer to this is that classical tragedy is not spoken but declaimed. In some ways, in performance, it is nearer to opera than to drama. This likewise creates enormous difficulties for audiences of the twentieth century; for even in France where a tradition in the speaking of classical tragedy and the management of alexandrines has been handed down from the days when Molière's company, after his death, combined with the company of the Hôtel de Bourgogne to form the Comédie Française, in spite of this living tradition French actors find it difficult to strike a medium between a tedious sing-song and a naturalistic rush, to give the verse its quality and yet to make it sound alive. Yes, it's very difficult even for the most experienced and gifted actors to play Racine; but when it's *achieved*, it's memorable. French classical tragedy has something in common with Greek sculpture and architecture. Outwardly it's still, even cold. But when you look more closely, or allow yourself to feel more perceptively, you become aware of the passions that lie behind the marvellous proportions of the work.

La Bruyère in the course of his *Caractères* made a just comparison between the two men. 'Corneille depicts people as they ought to be, Racine as they are; in the one there is much to admire and imitate, in the other there is what we may observe in others and experience in ourselves; the one elevates, astonishes, masters, instructs; the other delights, moves, touches, penetrates; everything that is most noble, beautiful, and exalted by reason is governed by the first; but the other handles things that are gratified and delicate in passion; in the former there are rules, precepts, maxims, in the latter taste and passion. One is more held by the plays of Corneille but more disturbed and affected by those of Racine.'

But when Louis XIV once asked this same La Bruyère who was the greatest writer of his age, the great critic answered,

'Sire, c'est Molière.'

BOOKS FOR FURTHER READING:

There is no English biography of Corneille. This is lamentable for his quiet life, divided between the two great cities of Paris and Rouen, the latter frequented with Spanish ships and sailors, is a colourful one.

There are two good lives of Molière, by John Palmer and H. Ashton.

Racine has been well served. I recommend lives by Mary Duclaux, and Geoffrey Brereton. François Mauriac's *Life* is also excellent but has not been translated.

An admirable critical work on all three dramatists is Martin Turnell's *The Classical Moment* a splendid discussion on the whole period.

Corneille and Racine have never been successfully translated; but there are many adequate versions of Molière, especially of his prose plays.

An extremely erudite but fascinating book which fills in much of the background to the original performances of these dramatists is John Lough's *Paris Theatre Audiences in the XVI and XVII Centuries.*

Examples of the critical writings of the French and Italian humanists together with the most important contributions to the controversy about *Le Cid* are to be found in *European Theories of Drama*, edited by Barrett H. Clark, available in an American paper-back edition.

The death of Molière is described in detail in my own *Great Moments in the Theatre.*

The best short eulogy of Racine I know is contained in *Books and Characters* by G. Lytton Strachey. This book also contains delightful chapters on Voltaire's tragedies and his relationship with Frederick the Great.

CHAPTER SEVEN

The Italian Dramatists: Goldoni and Gozzi

A NYONE LIVING in Florence between the years 1470 and 1530 would have found himself the fellow-citizen of Lorenzo Ghiberti, Donatello, Fra Angelico, Paolo Uccelli, Fra Fillipo Lippi, Pollaiuolo, Verrocchio, Botticelli, Ghirlandaio, Piero di Cosimo, Piero della Francesca, Leonardo da Vinci, Michaelangelo and Raphael, to name but the most outstanding of the most extraordinary group of artists ever to have lived in a single city at a single time.

Many of them enjoyed a versatile genius and set about mastering a number of different artistic disciplines. Few of them lived in reclusion. Florence was like a Greek city-state and her artists played their part in the life of the city.

Many of these artists found generous if sometimes unreliable patronage both in the Church, particularly from some of the Popes, and also from the despots who ruled these city-states, the Medicis of Florence, the Viscontis of Milan, the Estes of Ferrara and so on. Italy was not behind England and France in the prodigality of her religious spectacles and there can be little doubt that with the blessing of the blue Italian skies, the energy of her people, and their genius for visual splendour, the *Rappresentazioni sacre* must have exceeded in magnificence even the great French *Mystères* or the Spanish *Autos sacramentales*. And what worldly pieces they were

with their continual references to antiquity and their un-
saintly characters and strange parodies of men with names
like Coccodrillo, Scaramuccia, and Morgante.

Conditions seemed to be ideal for a tremendous efflores-
cence of the drama. But there were two destructive tendencies
at work. It's extremely disappointing to have to admit that
nothing kills the living quality of dramatic art so assuredly
as visual splendour. Elaborate scenery and ingenious machines
for moving it, opulent costumes and all the paraphernalia of
pageantry, excellent at the proper time, place and occasion,
tend to swamp actors and stultify the drama. The musical
theatre sometimes escapes death by suffocation through the
ability of opera singers to assert their presence against overwhelming odds by means of their powerful voices.

A more serious enemy of the drama was the attitude of the
humanists with their tyrannical dogmas and the sycophancy
of the writers who listened to them. These dogmas did help
to renew and reshape the sprawling drama of the later Middle
Ages but for every Racine there were hundreds of musty
pedants.

Dramatists and critics were so intoxicated by the culture
of antiquity, which nevertheless they did not understand at
all, that they were wholly unable to listen to the voice of their
own times, which is the only real inspiration of dramatic art,
and persevered in reviving Greek and Latin plays and then
imitating them. *Mandragola* by the Florentine diplomat Nic-
colo Machiavelli is the only example of a comedy displaying
the least sense of contemporary realism, and Machiavelli was
not a professional dramatist. Even the theatres were built on
what many architects took to be a Roman pattern and eventually proved to be suitable not for drama at all but for a
curiously hybrid theatrical form that came to be known as
opera.

And so in the course of the sixteenth century, when Lope
de Vega was still young and irrepressible and Shakespeare was

seeking to make his mark on Elizabethan audiences, Italian humanists suffocated the drama of their own country with misreadings of Aristotle and the Roman architect Vitruvius. They even succeeded in choking their own native language so that there was not a single Italian poet of outstanding quality between Petrarch who died in 1374 and Torquato Tasso who lived a short tormented life toadying at the courts of the despots two hundred years later.

This is not to condemn all the achievements of the classical scholars: it was only in the theatre that their influence was all but mortal. But while theory was choking popular culture, the despots were betraying the people themselves with their political ineptitude. Giving full rein to lust and sensuality, turning their scholars into arrogant but time-serving beggars, and their artists into sycophants, they let their country open to foreigners. They failed at every turn to establish their own republican ideals; and the people responded with a demonstration of astonishing independence, creating a popular drama that was lewd, satirical, vernacular, and entirely improvised.

We do not know whether this extraordinary theatrical movement, one of the most distinctive and vivacious ever to have erupted among civilised people, was the work of amateurs or professional. There are traces of both. Scholars are divided about its origins. There are some who see in the curious masked characters of the Improvised Comedy the descendants of those twisted curious characters of Plautus and Terence, believing that throughout the time of imperial Rome, all through the Dark and Middle Ages, for over fifteen hundred years, actors roamed Europe, preserving the tradition of an earthy improvised style of acting. Well, the similarities are striking; but then the Italians of the sixteenth century were deliberately reviving everything they could find of the old Roman culture. For present purposes it doesn't matter. The companies of the Commedia dell' Arte became celebrated throughout Europe.

It was an actor's theatre. Actors ransacked the literary drama, books of tales, every possible source for a good story, and then added their own words and actions. Even then they did not find, or they certainly did not choose, stories 'of their own time'; for this is a skill which marks a real writer. But having agreed upon their scenario they then adapted it for their own purposes by transforming the original characters of the story into the characters which they were accustomed to act. For Italian comedians had no use for versatility: they created a type and acted it throughout their lives. And these types came to be known as 'masks' from the half-masks worn by the comic characters.

But in these masks there was a certain contemporary realism. They were what the psychologists call archetypes of the characters that were to be seen in the streets of any Italian city. There was the swaggering and boastful Spanish Capitano; the Doctor from Bologna, where there had been a school of medicine for many centuries, full of Latin tags and pedantry; Pantalone who was a business man, a Venetian magnifico, and a lecher into the bargain with a sharp eye for pretty girls, and there was always a pair of lovers. But it was among the servants that we find the most lively and celebrated characters particularly the one that has become the most famous theatrical figure in the world, Arlecchino, or Harlequin, on whom the complicated intrigues of the plot usually turned.

So they travelled throughout Italy and all over Europe, these Pantalones and Arlecchinos, Cocodrillos, Morgantes and Columbines, taking their ancient names with them, setting up their simple stages in the market-places or even in the great halls of the nobility. And while from the scenario of a story that was pinned up in the wings of their simple stages these strange and colourful characters created their own play as they went along, Harlequin becomes the personification of theatrical invention; his hat becomes a pudding-basin and his slap-stick a horse. He turns his master into his slave and himself into the man-in-the-moon. He rides the wind and flies to the sun on a piece of thistle-down. He laughs with one side of his face and cries with the other. And when he is dying of hunger he tries to eat his toes and only succeeds in tickling himself into uncontrollable laughter.

At its best the Commedia dell' Arte must have provided a matchless experience. At its worst it was obscene, stereotyped, repetitive, and badly lacking the regenerative qualities of a poetic text. Of the strength of popular reaction against it in the eighteenth century we have no means of knowing. What we do know is that Carlo Goldoni (1707-1793) made it his life's work to establish the precedence of the dramatist in the Italian theatre and to create a written national drama.

Goldoni was a Venetian and in Venice he spent a large part of his life. Venice is not a city like Amsterdam, intersected by canals as other cities are by roads, but a group of islands set in the middle of a lagoon and joined to the mainland by a causeway. Through the midst of these islands twists the Grand Canal dividing the city into two almost equal halves.

It is said that Venice is not a typically Italian city. In the fifteenth century when the other city-states were on terms of jealous hostility with each other, Venice was the centre of an Empire that included some of the Aegean islands, Cyprus, Crete, and parts of the Dalmatian coast. She held a virtual monopoly of the overland trade with the east and her merchants were among the richest men in Europe. Her mercantile supremacy in the Mediterranean brought her continually into armed conflict with Turkey which had been for many centuries the leading country in the Middle East. But during the sixteenth and seventeenth centuries when the cities on the mainland began to lose their independence to foreign powers, and the small Venetian republic was unable to maintain her own political sovereignty, her Empire fell away and with it her political independence.

But the consequences of her wealth remained; for besides

the rare beauty of her setting, Venice was a city of many fine buildings, museums, churches, cathedrals, theatres. She was well, though autocratically, governed and celebrated throughout Europe for the gaiety of her carnivals, masques and balls. The rich went to Venice as now to Monte Carlo to gamble away their last penny in an atmosphere of faded magnificence and dying splendour. The city had the reputation, which Paris was later to acquire, as the home of gay but perhaps rather irresponsible people. It was all bad for politics but excellent for tourism.

One of the principal sources for the facts of Goldoni's life are his own *Memoires* which he wrote in French in his old age. Scholars have discovered that he was much less interested in telling the truth about himself than creating the character of a gay and carefree wag who might have stepped out of one of his own gay comedies. He gives us a picture of irresponsible youth, well-to-do parents, and a great reluctance to study. His father, a doctor, was addicted to theatre-going and encouraged this interest in his son. At the age of eleven Carlo wrote a comedy, set out on a tour of northern Italy for the sake of his education, but found himself unable to resist the lure of the theatres. It makes a good story. At the age of fourteen he ran away from school and spent a time in the company of a group of 'strolling players' 'on the road'. (I don't know why the word 'strolling' is always applied to actors on tour. In those days they would have travelled on horseback or in a cart. If they had been obliged to walk they would have trudged, not strolled.) And so, during his youth, he rolled happily from job to job, until by the time he was thirty he had been a law student, a diplomat of the Venetian government, a lawyer, a playwright, and enjoyed more experiences with attractive young ladies than most of us do in a lifetime—if he is to be believed.

One of the striking features of Goldoni's *Memoirs* is his reluctance to speak ill of anything or anybody. Consequently he says little in condemnation of the Commedia dell' Arte for which he seems to have had a good deal of contempt. Nor is he strikingly clear over his own determination to reform the Italian theatre by creating a literary drama. Indeed he wrote a good many plays before he began to realise that this was his true métier. This may have been because he started off writing the wrong kind of plays: classical tragedies in the manner of the commedia erudita and libretti for the composers of opera, a form that was becoming not merely popular but the 'rage' in Italy of that time. (Opera had been originated in the fifteen-nineties by a group of young men who realising that Athenian tragedy had had an almost continuous musical accompaniment were experimenting with methods of composing neo-Greek tragedy. So, since operas began as classical tragedies set to music, tragedy remained a popular subject for librettists right up until its hey-day in the nineteenth century.)

Between 1734 and 1743 Goldoni lived in Venice, employed as Consul for the Genoese government. During this time he wrote about thirty plays and libretti, most of them for a troupe that was led by a certain Sacchi, a celebrated Truffaldino. But he still was not writing with dedicated passion. In 1744 he even decided to abandon drama in order to practise law in Pisa; but a perceptive manager called Medebach recognising his talent lured him back to Venice and established him as a full-time professional dramatist at the Teatro de Sant' Angelo, one of the seven fiercely competitive Venetian theatres. The year was 1747. Goldoni was forty. His contract provided for him to write eight comedies a year and two opera libretti, to rewrite old comedies, assist at rehearsals, and accompany the troupe on tour. Though he got his pound of flesh Medebach gave invaluable encouragement to Goldoni at a difficult time in his career.

That Goldoni was slow to recognise his own talent was probably due to the utter lack of introspection in his character. He had little interest in psychology or man's deeper emotions. He was inventive without being imaginative, swiftly observant without being perceptive. While it is perfectly true to say that he was a reformer or a transformer, this is to make him sound more of an original genius than he was. We can see the extent of his reforms in one of his charming early plays, *Il servitore di due padroni* (*The Servant of Two Masters*, 1740). For here he has taken a typical script of the improvised comedy and developed it into a written play. No gigantic creative effort perhaps, but indicative of his felicitous and unpretentious gifts.

And so he persisted in trying to free the drama from what he considered to be the anarchy of improvisation. In his next plays he lessened the importance of the improvised characters, the masks, and gave the lovers, who had a subsidiary role in genuine improvised performances, a dominating part in the plot. For many years he continued to use the four main masks, Harlequin, Brighella, Pantalone and the Doctor, but never again did he make them protagonists. Comparing *The Servant of Two Masters* with *Il Bugiardo* (*The Liar*), we find Harlequin, the most demonically zestful character in dramatic literature, reduced to the role of an unimportant servant.

During the next fourteen years Goldoni wrote about a hundred comedies and a large number of libretti. During the theatrical season 1750-1751 he made a wager that he would write and produce sixteen comedies in the single season. He won. His first was a sort of testament of faith called *The Comic Theatre*, rather similar to Molière's *Critique de l'école des femmes*; he went on to write some of his best plays, *The Liar*, *La Bottega di Caffè* (*The Coffee House*), and *Il Moliere* (*Molière*).

In the next ten years Goldoni maintained the output of plays that was required by his various contracts. Some he wrote in Italian, some in the Venetian dialect; most of them were based on some aspect of Venetian society, many were closely observed and few are not bubbling with high spirits. Those most likely to be found in English translation are *La Locandiera* (*Mine Hostess* or *The Mistress of the Inn*, 1753), a play which in the role of Mirandolina contains one of his most successful pieces of character-drawing; *L'Impresario della Smirne* (*The Impresario from Smyrna*, 1761), an amusing play about life in a theatrical company *La Buona Moglie* (*The Good Wife*, 1749), a charming comedy of sexual intrigue; and *Un Curioso Accidente* (*A Curious Accident*, 1757).

I must warn you that you may read these plays with a sense of disappointment. The décor in some way has become over familiar. We've had too many plays that turn upon sexual entanglements involving people in whom we are never greatly interested. The pattern of the intrigues is repetitive. If we compare Goldoni's plays with Molière's, which some critics have been enthusiastic enough to do, we see how shallow they are; if we compare them with Sheridan, how lacking in wit. Yet they remain plays of supreme good humour, delightfully observed plays, plays of small but amusing people who stroll through the streets of Venice with an eye for a pretty girl, arguing with the gondoliers, and stopping for coffee in a shop that's a centre of local intrigue. Goldoni was the opposite of a man like Strindberg who had genius but small talent. He had enormous talent and in no way did he demonstrate it more clearly than in his ability to write within himself, to understand and accept the nature of his talent and develop it to the full.

Goldoni was not without his enemies. Many were simply jealous. There were aristocrats who detested his kindly liberalism; for while there is no satire in Goldoni there is a constant readiness to jest at the quirks of the aristocracy. There were the plain reactionaries who regretted the passing of the Improvised Comedy. With something of all these complaints, and the iron deep within his soul, was a certain Count Carlo Gozzi. He was the sixth child in a family of twelve. He had an irresponsible and reckless father and was inadequately educated by a number of priests who were all dismissed for intriguing with the maidservants. As a boy he wrote and read prolifically and when his home broke up he joined the army. Here he had some success as an amateur actor in entertaining the officers' mess. Three years later he returned home and found the house and family, his brothers and sisters, stifled by debt and all involved in one kind of intrigue or another. So he embarked upon a period of litigation to redeem the family fortunes and clear up the mess. In his little spare time he dabbled in literature.

He was a far from easy man, morose, sardonic, solitary, nicknamed 'The Bear', in every respect the antithesis of the gay and easy-going Goldoni.

It was the growing custom in Italy, as it had been in France, in the seventeenth and eighteenth centuries, for intelligent and well-meaning people to form various kinds of salons and academies for social, artistic and literary purposes. In Venice Gozzi had been to the fore in establishing the Accademia Granellesca, which has the ironic meaning of Academy of Simpletons. Its aims we have heard before: to promote the study of the best Italian authors, and to develop a pure and simple style of speech and prose. Among the butts of the Academy were the heavy and verbose tragedies of certain contemporary dramatists, which is understandable, and Goldoni, who was disliked for many things, not least for his reputed susceptibility to the influence of Molière. (*The Liar* was in fact an adaptation of Corneille's *Le Menteur*, but Goldoni admired Molière and learnt French in order to read his plays in the original.)

But the clash between Gozzi and Goldoni was as much a clash of temperaments as of principles. Gozzi led the attack through the legitimate channels of literary criticism, vilifying Goldoni's plays in the Venetian journals, in pamphlets and poems. This was in 1756. But when the Frenchman Voltaire

threw his enormous prestige behind Goldoni, Gozzi decided
to challenge his rival on his own ground, that of the drama.
It's a part of the supreme irony of the man and of the situation that he should have written and made a success of a story
that was little more than a popular fairy-tale, *L'Amore
delle tre melarancie, (The Love of the Three Oranges*, 1761). As
for the writing, it's a scenario of a dozen pages which he gave
to the great Sacchi and which the famous Truffaldino seems
to have performed with enormous skill. But author and actors
worked into the piece the most swingeing contempt for
Goldoni and his fellow dramatists. And in 1761 Goldoni found
himself being laughed at. His actions suggest how much he
suffered, for in his refusal to speak ill of anyone he records
nothing of how deeply the growing attacks must have dis-
tressed him. It was barely three months after the first production of *The Love of the Three Oranges* that he received an invitation from the French ambassador to visit Paris and write
plays for *Les Comédiens du roi de la troupe Italienne*. He took
from March till September to decide that he would accept; in
the following February he gave the farewell performance of
the last play he wrote in Italy, and on April 15th he left
Venice, arriving in Paris in August.

Gozzi was left victorious. He went on to write more
'theatrical fables' as he called them, strange fanciful pieces
which had a great vogue among German romantics in the
nineteenth century. They were all played by Sacchi's company but when we come to read them it's distressing to find
how little has been left to improvisation and how much of the
dialogue has been written in. He wrote the last of them in
1765. It was over forty years before he died. They must
have gone very slowly. We have a last picture of him sitting
with Sacchi in Venetian coffee-shops and lamenting the death
of the Comedy of Masks.

Oh yes, and in his old age he wrote his Memoirs, a satirical
book, like his life, to which he gave the title, *Useless Memoirs*

of Carlo Gozzi (Memorie inutili) written by himself and published 'in humility'. An unhappy man of whom the great stream of posterity has taken little account.

Goldoni was getting on for sixty when he arrived in Paris. He found what must have been a tantalizing theatrical situation. Though invited to write for the Italians he seems to have been critical of their skill.

We last mentioned them when in 1658 Molière was obliged to share the Théâtre du Petit-Bourbon. In 1680, after the death of Molière, Louis XIV formed the Comédie Française by amalgamating the existing French companies and gave them residence in a new theatre in the Rue Guénégaud. The Comédie Italienne then moved to the Théâtre de l'Hôtel de Bourgogne, now vacated. Though required by their licence to play in Italian they took every opportunity to introduce French songs and dialogue into their performances, and in time were giving whole plays in French. Eventually their impudence ran away with them and when in 1697 they affronted Madame de Maintenant, the King's mistress, they were banished. The death of Louis XIV gave them an opportunity to return and in 1716 they established themselves once again in the Hôtel de Bourgogne under the leadership of the distinguished actor Luigi Riccoboni who in every way restored the status and the standing of the company. But the Italian style was now right out of favour and they were even more dependant upon French plays. Before their banishment they had been well served by Jean-François Regnard (1655-1709) with whose comedy *Le Joueur* (*The Gambler*, 1696) they had had a great success. Now they gathered round them a new group of dramatists of whom the most outstanding by far was Pierre Carlet de Chamblain de Marivaux (1688-1763). In 1720 they had a great success with his third comedy, *Arlequin poli par l'amour*. The title sets the tone of the thing; a subtle and lively mixture of Italian comedy, full of physical vitality, with the graceful style and sophistication of the French comedy of manners. It's a strangely attractive genre, nostalgic, brittle, heavily scented, intensely stylish, surprisingly sensitive to psychological movement, and a little decadent. Although the best known of the plays of Marivaux is *Le Jeu de l'amour et du hasard* (*The Game of Love and Chance*, 1730), my own favourite, a play that strikes exactly the style I am describing, is *La Seconde Surprise de l'amour*, 1727). Both were played by the Italians.

It was for the Italians that Marivaux, a Frenchman, wrote his best plays. Goldoni, an Italian, wrote his best for the French. In 1764 the Italians still preferred a scenario to a play with lines that had to be learnt. But Goldoni continued his reforms and although the Italians played one of his new comedies, *Il Ventaglio*, (*The Fan,*, 1763), one that is now considered to be among his best, he notes that he wrote it in short scenes through the inability of the Italians to sustain anything longer.

Settled in Paris his relations with the Italian actors became strained. He made up his mind to return to Venice but was offered a post at the court of Versailles teaching Italian to the children of Louis XV. Then in 1770 his ambition was fulfilled: *Le Bourru bienfaisant*, which he had written in French, was successfully staged at the Comédie Française. It was an amiable play of the kind which the French wrote admirably themselves but is nothing to be compared with his best Venetian comedies.

In his *Memoires* he records amusing conversations with Jean Jacques Rousseau and Denis Diderot. He lived to see the outbreak of the French Revolution. But by that time his *Memoires* had already been published and we have no means of knowing how that passionate eruption of human emotion stirred his happy and easy-going Italian temperament.

BOOKS FOR FURTHER READING:

The standard works on the Commedia dell' Arte are Pierre Duchartre's *The Italian Comedy*, translated by Randolph Weaver and K. M. Lea's *Italian Popular Comedy*. Both text and pictures are excellent in Allardyce Nicoll's *Mimes Masks and Miracles*.

The best study of the period I have found in English is Vernon Lee's finely written *Studies of the Eighteenth Century in Italy*. There are brilliant chapters on Gozzi, Goldoni, and many other aspects of the Italian scene.

Goldoni's *Memoirs* have been translated into English by John Black.

There are good English translations of many of Goldoni's comedies. *La Locandiera* appears as *The Mistress of the Inn*, *The Coquettish Innkeeper*, *Mine Hostess* and *Mirandolina*. There may be other variations.

This play, together with *The Fan* and *The Boors* have been published together in a book that contains an interesting introduction on Goldoni by Professor Gabriele Baldini.

There are two English biographies of Goldoni, one by H. C. Chatfield-Taylor, and another called *Goldoni and the Venice of his Time* by Joseph Spencer Kennard.

Gozzi's *Memoirs* have been translated by J. A. Symonds.

Of his fables *Il Mostro Turchino* (*The Blue Monster*) has been translated by Professor E. J. Dent and *Il Re Cervo* (*King Stag*) by Karl Wildman via the French. *The Love of the Three Oranges* and *Turandot* have been turned into operas by Prokoviev and Puccini respectively.

The Theatre of Marivaux by Kenneth McKee is an excellent critical introduction to the plays of this seductive dramatist but lacks biographical material. In a pointedly worded introduction, Jean-Louis Barrault, who has made some successful productions of Marivaux, describes his plays as having 'the cruelty of the sadist, the material bitterness of the bourgeois, the elegance of the aristocrat, the indignation of the revolutionary, and the droll wisdom of the man in the street.'

CHAPTER EIGHT

The German Dramatists:
Goethe and Schiller

W E NOW MOVE from the seventeenth to the eighteenth century; from the Mediterranean across the mountains into Central Europe. To find at last a German dramatist among the great European writers is a sign that Germany was at last achieving some kind of political and social stability. Goethe was born in 1749. The date is a little more than a hundred years after the Treaty of Westphalia which, by ending the Thirty Years War, put a stop to a hideous period of slaughter and destruction. It is reckoned that of a population of about thirty million, a third lost their lives and a good many more than that their property. The land that is now Germany was decimated.

In the eighteenth century there was no such thing as a German state or nation although it is now customary to see, in the shifting policies of Prussia, the beginnings of German nationalism. The land consisted of about three hundred princedoms, principalities, kingdoms, dukedoms, and electorates, amongst which the only states of political consequence were Prussia in the north, Saxony in the centre, and Bavaria in the south. The ruling kings, princes, dukes, electors, and petty potentates were for the most part what we should now call benevolent despots, though both their benevolence and their despotism varied according to their several temperaments.

They were the counterpart of the Italian Medicis, Sforzas and Viscontis. They ruled, for the most part, without constitutions; their word was law; but some of them were genuine liberals with high cultural ideals and a progressive policy towards social legislation.

The dominating countries of Europe in the eighteenth century were France and England; France because the aggressive foreign policy of Louis XIV had been substantiated by an intellectual and artistic renaissance which had put a high premium upon French culture; England because her political philosophers talked remarkably good sense about the responsibilities of a monarch towards his subjects, capital punishment, education, the study of science, the importance of a lucid literary style, and eloquent conversation. The dominating European figures in the world of ideas were Descartes and Diderot from the one country, Locke, Hobbes and Hume from the other. This was all fairly healthy. The artistic giants were Voltaire and Shakespeare. This led to a good many difficulties as we shall see.

Generally speaking the European trend towards rationalism was known in Germany as 'die Aufklärung', the enlightenment. And it was French influence that showed the way. German theatres gave many French plays, people who considered themselves fashionable spoke French in preference to their own language. The German sovereigns tried to make their courts as Frenchified as possible. Frederick the Great of Prussia, one of the great German nationalists, called his exquisite palace in Potsdam Sans Souci, and filled it with French books in fine French leather bindings, which are still there to be admired. Even after he had eventually rounded upon his French advisers, turned out his friend Voltaire, made war upon France and soundly beaten her, he still called in French civil servants to administer his taxes.

Theatrically speaking the country had to start pretty well, as we say, from scratch. At the beginning of the century theatrical conditions were deplorable. By the middle of the century there were perhaps eight regular companies 'on the road' covering German speaking Europe from Switzerland to Russia by way of Austria. None of them had a permanent theatre and the princes had not yet begun to extend to them their patronage.

Because they deserve our respect, and because it will help to make clear the contribution of Goethe and Schiller to the theatre, let me mention the names of the men and women who contributed to the creation of the German national theatre.

In the first half of the century the most outstanding figure was Johann Christoph Gottsched (1700-1766), a critic and unsuccessful playwright who was all too successful in persuading the best companies to base their repertory on the French classical drama. His theories were strongly supported in practice by the leading actress-manager of the time, Karoline Neuber (1697-1760), who established standards of acting and production, and brought, for the first time, prestige and status to the German theatre.

One of the most ambitious projects of the time was the attempt to found a National Theatre in Hamburg. This effort was energetically supported by Gotthold Lessing, a brilliant man who achieved fame both as the author of plays like *Minna von Barnhelm* (1767) and some of the most interesting dramatic criticisms ever to have been written. These criticisms made into a famous collection now called *The Hamburg Dramaturgy*, helped to create some sort of proportion between the competing claims of Shakespeare and the French classical dramatists.

Other important pioneers were Konrad Ackermann, who was closely associated with the theatre in Hamburg; Konrad Eckhoff, who acted frequently with Ackermann's company and was the first German actor to give serious thought to the problem of training actors; and perhaps the greatest of them all, Friedrich Schröder, actor, manager and producer who did for the German theatre and German acting very much what Goethe was to do for the drama.

By the second part of the century these men and women had succeeded in establishing certain principles upon which a national theatre should be based, namely, that artistic as well as commercial values were important for assessing the success of a production; that actors should be trained and paid properly; and that the German drama should be enlisted in the cause of the 'enlightenment'.

These ideas first began to take root in Prussia, which included the cities of Berlin and Hamburg, and in Saxony of which the cultural centres were Dresden and Leipzig. They were welcomed by those of the three hundred potentates who felt themselves to be apogees of the enlightenment, but not by the rest.

Unfortunately the intellectual movement towards sweetness and light was bedevilled by the most sinister religious tensions, which had survived from the Thirty Years War. In a largely Protestant population there were many dissident groups composed of people who wished to increase the element of personal religious experience in Christianity, believing that there was too much ritual and too little prayer and meditation.

This rather emotional movement became involved with the gathering passions of the people towards nationalism. In an attempt to discover and create their own identity as Germans, poets recalled the national myths and legends and imbued them with highly charged emotional overtones rather as happened in the nineteen-thirties. And so the two movements played upon each other: on the one side mysticism and personal religious experience, and on the other, political nationalism. The outcome was sentimentality and hysteria. The emotional temperature of the country rose. Its literature became dark, passionate, and hysterical. Against the classical rationalism of the Aufklärung there developed a movement known as 'Sturm und Drang' (roughly, storm and stress). The leaders were a group of young men who wrote poetry and plays which they thought to be Shakespearian but which in fact are windy, dull and emotionally chaotic. Not very many people today have heard of, let alone read, the play that gave its title to the movement—*Sturm und Drang*; or could name its author—Friedrich Klinger; or the names of his associates, playwrights as poor as he, Johann Lenz and Heinrich Wagner. Their plays were cheered to the echo by audiences for whom *Hamlet* and *Othello* were too powerful to be endured! And all this while a certain number of priests and theologians attacked the princes whose courts were centres of the enlightenment for being puppets of French culture and offering delicate pedantries and dilettantism in place of an indigenous German culture.

This was the situation into which Goethe and Schiller were born.

Johann Wolfgang von Goethe (the 'von' was a kind of knighthood he received later in life) was born at Frankfurt-am-Main in 1749. He had excellent parents who fostered his natural intelligence and love of learning. Intending him to be a lawyer his father sent him to Leipzig, one of the most cultured cities in Germany, where he came into contact with all the passions of the day. Illness brought him back to Frankfurt in 1768 when he was still only nineteen. Even at that age he was profoundly interested in alchemy, astrology, philosophy, French literature and Shakespeare and showing something of the universality that made him one of the great Europeans of the age. He had already written some superb lyric poetry inspired by an early love-affair, and in the next few years, between 1770 and 1776 he went on to write the historic drama *Goetz von Berlichingen* which made him the hero of the Sturm und Drang movement—Klinger's play did not appear for another three years—the first draft of *Faust*, his first novel *Die Leiden des jungen Werther* (translated as *The Sorrows of Werther*) and three more plays *Clavigo*, *Stella* and *Egmont*.

Goetz von Berlichingen is not an attractive play to read. It's a windy, sprawling, unkempt, anarchical affair chiefly interesting for its hero who for all his apparent defence of liberty, strikes one as being the strong-armed blustering nationalist who 150 years later would have been a militant Nazi.

Clavigo and *Stella*, one a historical, the other a domestic tragedy, are both more impressive to see performed than to read. Goethe spent no great time on either of them and it's unfortunate that the second and far more conventional version of *Stella* is always printed in preference to the original version which in Goethe's own day was condemned as immoral. How the practice of suppressing books and plays that are thought to shock or offend runs like a curse through the history of literature and drama!

Egmont is by far the best of Goethe's early plays and it is easy to understand Beethoven's enthusiasm for it and its continual revival upon the German stage. The fight of the heroic Dutch leader Egmont against the oppression and ruthless treachery of the Spanish Alva makes a tremendous theme. We are not asked to sympathise with rhetorical heroic gestures, but the calculated courage of a democratic leader against a military dictatorship. The play contains many scenes of outstanding dramatic impact.

By the year 1775 Goethe, at the age of twenty-six, had become one of the most celebrated men in Germany, famous for his achievements, for his explosive character, and the range of his mind. It was in this year that Karl August, the Duke of Saxe-Weimar, who at the age of eighteen had just taken over the government of this tiny duchy from his mother Anna Amalia, invited Goethe, whom he had met two years previously, to come and live in Weimar.

Weimar in 1775 was a small and sleepy little town in

Thuringia with six thousand inhabitants, most of them living off the land, and a lively court. Indeed, while the need for brevity compels one to emphasise the serious side of Goethe's development, it is as well to establish that this godlike young man was by no means averse to joining the Duke's frequent drinking bouts and indeed for many years kept up a supply of masquerades, burlesques, and satirical shows for the entertainment of the young Duke and his courtiers.

The ostensible reason for the invitation was to direct theatrical performances in the small theatre that had been built in the old redoutensaal or ball-room. Goethe enjoyed acting and the Duke had offered him a free hand. But the Duke was clearly quick to see the efforts he must make to keep so prodigious a figure as Goethe in so small a town as Weimar and wasted little time in appointing him to his privy council. The President was affronted and only prevented from resigning by the greatest exertions of the Duke and his mother the dowager Duchess.

Goethe however faced his responsibilities conscientiously and soon found himself directly responsible for agriculture, mining, forestry and even the treasury in the little Duchy; not to mention the management of the theatre where from time to time he played a leading role himself. Even so he continued to write prolifically. From this period, 1775-1786 come many of his finest poems, *Wilhelm Meisters theatralische Sendung* (sendung means mission) which in 1796 appeared as *Wilhelm Meister Lehrjahre*; and two plays in verse, *Tasso* and *Iphigenie auf Tauris*.

He was now due for 'leave' and the Duke permitted him to go to Italy for two years. Strictly speaking it was not until his return that he completed the plays already mentioned. Indeed their qualities and defects clearly emerge from the fact that he worked on them as dramatic poems rather than as stage dramas over a number of years.

It is difficult to understand what interested Goethe in the

curious episode of the rescue of Iphigenie from the distant land of Tauris by her brother Orestes at the end of the Trojan war; but the life of the Italian poet, Torquato Tasso, who was continually obliged to grub around for patronage among the Italian princes, and who ended his life in the unhappiest state of mental collapse, is not only moving and fascinating on its own account, but one that has striking similarities with Goethe's own relationship with the Duke.

The form of the plays makes clear that he had by now completely rejected the Shakespearian mood in which he had written *Goetz* and become far more interested, not so much in the French classical drama, as in the original and authentic classical drama of the Athenian dramatists. I am sure that these great dramatic poems are an expression of his reversion against the vulgar and knock-about nature of popular theatrical art of which he saw plenty at Weimar. Indeed many of Goethe's most serious works are scientific and I fancy he was appalled by the hopelessly anarchical and unscientific methods by which actors developed their roles and got their effects. He says so repeatedly in his letters and implies as much in his *Rules for Actors* which he published many years later and which reduce histrionic art almost to a form of behaviour.

Johann Christoph Friedrich Schiller (1759-1805) was exactly ten years younger than Goethe. The son of an army surgeon he was sent to be educated in a military academy in the important town of Stuttgart, the capital of another small princedom which was ruled by Karl Eugen, Duke of Würtemburg. This Duke, whose picture shows him to have a plump, sour, and unimaginative face, was by way of being a bit of a despot, and a very different kind of duke from Goethe's master. Schiller, though destined at first to go into the Church and then to become a doctor, soon showed that he was interested in nothing but literature, and like many another young man before and since it was the drama that first attracted him.

After some experiments with Biblical themes he came across a short story in a magazine that caught his imagination. He set to work to turn it into a play. The year was 1777. The youth of Germany was full of Goethe's *Goetz* and Klinger's *Sturm und Drang*. Schiller was young, emotional, and imaginative. *The Robbers* is a thoroughbred of the period. It took Schiller four years to write for he was a student at the military academy and since his tutors despised literature, the hospital was the only place where he could find the necessary quiet. When he had at last finished the play he used the good offices of a publisher to send it to Wolfgang von Dalberg, the director of the National Theatre in Mannheim. It was finally produced on January 13, 1782, with the great August Iffland in the leading role of Karl Moor. The play was received with the hysterical shrieks and groans that are reserved today for 'pop' singers of tender years. Such was the impression made by the performance that to many people it seemed to create the possibility of a new heaven and a new earth!

The Duke did not approve the notoriety achieved by one of his students and ordered Schiller to submit any further literary efforts to him for censorship. Schiller rebelled. When the play was revived he broke out of the Academy by night, and went to Mannheim (in the neighbouring state of the Palatinate), to see it acted. On his return he was confined to barracks. This was too much. He escaped from the Academy and went again to Mannheim in search of a job in the theatre. Dalberg did not immediately take him and it was a year before he got the post he coveted. His second play *Fiesco* was then produced but was another failure. A few months later, his third, *Kabale und Liebe* (*Intrigue and Love*, though the words are usually reversed) went rather better. But he never really came to terms with the management of the Mannheim theatre and a year later he was again seeking accommodation among his friends.

In 1787 he completed one of the most famous of his plays,

the great historical drama of *Don Carlos*. While it contains scenes of tremendous power that rightly give it a permanent position upon the German stage, it has all the faults of a play that has been written over a number of years. It's a vast sprawling shapeless play. Its theme is continually shifting. Schiller was not only uncertain about the kind of play he wanted to write but lacked the concentration necessary to solve the tremendous problems he had given himself. But apart from its own qualities it's an important step on the way to *Wallenstein*.

Schiller had become a well-known name to the enterprising young Karl August of Weimar, and in 1787, while Goethe was in Italy, the Duke invited the young dramatist to Weimar. The upshot of the visit was that Schiller got a job as Professor of History in the neighbouring university of Jena. Goethe had a hand in the appointment but remarks in one of his letters on the irony of recommending a young man for a post on the strength of a play like *The Robbers* which stood for all that he now most detested in the theatre.

In 1791 Schiller became ill with consumption and remained in poor health until his death in 1805. The generosity of a number of princes and patrons relieved him of financial worries but he continued a sick man. From 1787 until 1794 he wrote some important historical works and a large amount of fine poetry. From the study of history he turned to philosophy and then to aesthetics, finally writing to Goethe and inviting him to contribute to a literary journal he was editing. The two men met and the result of a long correspondence and deepening friendship was that in 1799 Schiller and his wife went to live permanently in Weimar.

The ducal theatre was still under Goethe's management. The greatest of all German authors was spending a large amount of his time planning a repertory which included besides his own and Schiller's plays and the highly successful operas of the brilliant young Wolfgang Amadeus Mozart, many of the most rubbishy and worthless pieces of the day.

The arrival of Schiller in Weimar made all this much more worth while. Their mutual interest in the theatre had begun in 1796 during one of Schiller's visits when the company occupying the theatre had been led by Iffland. Schiller was enthralled by his acting but disgusted by the plays in which, on the whole, he was appearing. On his return home he wrote a curious satirical poem called *Shakespeares Schatten* in which he laments the absence of a heroic poetic theatre. The poem gave rise to a lengthy correspondence with Goethe on the state of the German drama..

So when Schiller arrived in Weimar the two men found themselves in control of a theatre where they could work out their ideas; for as long as they supplied a certain number of popular plays to entertain the locals—an important consideration—there were opportunities for them to experiment.

Both men were passionately interested in philosophy. Their heads were stuffed with ideas, and ideas about ideas which they wanted to work into their plays. (With Goethe the outcome was that curious poetical philosophical work of genius, *Faust*.) Schiller was particularly interested in the patterns of history, both by training, by natural inclination, and because it was the *zeitgeist* of his epoch. Both men wished to reform the German drama. They had both wholly repudiated the quasi-Shakespearian style which they had indulged in *Goetz* and *Egmont*, in *The Robbers* and *Don Carlos*. They were searching for a poetic drama with the clarity and strong clean lines of Attic tragedy. This is clearly exemplified in *Iphigenia* and *Tasso*. Indeed it's almost disconcerting to find the two men at this moment of their lives translating Racine's *Phèdre* (the work of Schiller) and Voltaire's ridiculous tragedies *Mahomet* and *Tancrède* (that of Goethe). Too many ideas about the way to handle his material are not always helpful to a dramatist. The problem of varying his theatrical forms can rarely have entered Shakespeare's head. Goldoni was always perfectly clear what he wanted to do: so were Corneille, Molière and Racine, and they went ahead and did it. Schiller with no less genius than any of them was not able to settle down and write within an accepted and acceptable dramatic form. On the single occasion on which he does so, in the great *Wallenstein* trilogy, using with considerable discipline and mastery the historical poetic form he had experimented with in *Don Carlos*, he writes an indisputable masterpiece—three, in fact—for each of the plays that compose the Wallenstein trilogy is a masterpiece: *Wallensteins Lager* (camp), *Die Piccolomini* and *Wallensteins Tod* (death). In a better world than ours they would hold the stage of every civilized community.

The Wallenstein trilogy was completed in 1799. He wrote four more plays, each of a very different kind. *Maria Stuart*, an idealised portrait of the Queen of Scots during the last weeks of her life, is a play of character, overlaid with the heavy trappings of German romanticism in the form of scenes of tremendous theatrical effectiveness but a corresponding sense of artificiality. *Die Jungfrau von Orleans* (*The Maid of Orleans*, 1801) is a curious attempt to retell the story of Joan of Arc in the form of a classical tragedy with Johanna depicted as something between a virginal country maiden and an avenging fury, the facts of her life so violently distorted for theatrical ends as barely to be recognisable.

In *Die Braut von Messina* (*The Bride of Messina*) Schiller attempts to imitate closely the form of classical tragedy, even to the use of a chorus. The story is his own but the incidents of which this dark tragedy is compounded are stale enough. It is a calamity that with his tireless will to experiment and a sublime power of language, Schiller could not escape the imaginative limitations of his time.

His last play, *Wilhelm Tell*, owes its popularity almost wholly to its juvenile heroics.

Schiller died at the age of forty-six, full of ideas for future plays and promising as much as he had achieved.

During the last six years of Schiller's life, when he had devoted himself almost wholly to writing plays, Goethe had never lost interest in the theatre although he had written nothing of consequence himself in the way of plays. Then in 1808, three years after Schiller's death, he completed and published the first part of *Faust*. (The even more extraordinary second part was published posthumously.) This is the most remarkable of all the experiments of these two extraordinary men. It is difficult to know how to assess such a brilliantly hybrid affair. No one would class it as drama along with *Agamemnon* or *Hamlet*, yet its poetic and intellectual distinction leaps across the footlights when it is adequately performed upon the stage, and make it among the most remarkable products of human genius. Goethe was not living in a world that was striving to make civilization out of chaos, as the world of which Corneille was writing, nor one that contained such violent religious and political animosities as Shakespeare knew: Goethe was both a product of the eighteenth century and of 'sturm und drang'. He lived through the vast spectacular pageant of the Napoleonic tragedy. In these various strands we can find something of the composure that gives *Tasso* its serenity, the violence of *Goetz*, the lyricism of the first part of *Faust* and the demonism of the second. Goethe, like Marlowe, drives to the frontiers of human experience to solve the problem of man's predicament which Napoleon had made a matter of such moment. And in doing so he strains dramatic form until the result, though superb, is hardly recognisable as drama.

The conclusion of Goethe's *Faust* is not a piece of fustian demonism as in Marlowe's play. There are in fact two endings. Faust's adventures end on a whimper. His death is recounted by four Grey Women, Want, Debt, Care, and Need. But Goethe's conclusion is a reaffirmation of faith in man. Here he voices both the spiritual confidence of the eighteenth century and the material assurance of the nineteenth. The translation is by Louis Macneice.

I have only galloped through the world
And clutched each lust and longing by the hair.
What did not please me I let go,
What flowed away I let it flow.
I have only felt, only fulfilled desire,
And once again desired and thus with power
Have stormed my way through life; first great and strong
Now moving savagely, prudently along.
This earthly cycle I know well enough.
Towards the Beyond the view has been cut off.
Fool—who directs that way his dazzled eye,
Contrives himself a double in the sky!
Let him look round him here, not stray beyond.
To a sound man this world must needs respond.
To roam into eternity is vain!
What he perceives he can attain.

And here for the purposes of comparison is the passage in the original German.

Ich bin nur durch die Welt gerannt;
Ein jed' Gelust ergriff ich bei den Harren.
Was nicht genugte, liesz ich fahren,
Was mir entwischte, liesz ich ziehn.
Ich habe nur begehrt und nur vollbracht
Und abermals gewunscht and so mit Macht
Mein Leben durch gesturmt; erst grosz und machtig,
Nun aber geht es weise, geht bedachtig.
Der Erdenkreis ist mir genug bekannt.
Nach druben ist die Aussicht uns verrant;
Thor, wer dorthin die Augen blinzend richtet,
Sich uber Wolken seinesgleichen dichtet!
Er stehe fest und sehe hier sich um.

Dem Tuchtigen ist diese Welt nicht stumm.
Was braucht er in die Ewigkeit zu schweifen!
Was er erkennt, laszt sich ergriefen.

BOOKS FOR FURTHER READING:

On Goethe there are some rather heavy biographies but little that's up-to-date or shows much interest in his theatrical enthusiasms. Yet the range of his writings is immense.

On Schiller there are biographies by Thomas Carlyle, H. W. Nevinson, and an excellent and more recent one by H. B. Garland.

While there exists a prodigious number of translations of Faust, especially of the first part, the rest of Goethe's plays and all Schiller's have been inadequately treated. This is not so much a comment on the translators, for German verse is very much easier to turn into English than French, Spanish or Italian, but on the continued unpopularity of German romanticism.

Goetz has been made the subject of a celebrated but contentious modern play, *Le Diable et le bon Dieu*, by Jean-Paul Sartre, translated by Kitty Black as *Lucifer and the Lord*.

It's interesting to compare Schiller's *Jungfrau* with Bernard Shaw's *Saint Joan* and Anouilh's *The Lark*.

W. H. Bruford's *Theatre Drama and Audience in Goethe's Germany* provides an admirable background to the whole period. H. B. Garland's *Storm and Stress* fills in some details.

But you'll have to learn German in any case in order to read the lyric poems of Goethe and Schiller in the original for they are miracles of their kind.

For the story of the first production of *The Robbers*, see my own *Great Moments in the Theatre*.

I might also add that Stephen Spender has made a translation of *Maria Stuart* which has been played at the Old Vic. The standard translation of the *Wallenstein* trilogy is by Coleridge.

Faust has had many excellent translators, notably Louis Macneice. Many other of the plays mentioned in this chapter have been translated but copies are scarce.

CHAPTER NINE

The Scandinavian Dramatists: Ibsen and Strindberg

I BSEN and Strindberg were Scandinavians, Ibsen the Norwegian being twenty-one years older than Strindberg the Swede. The differences both of their characters and their plays are more pronounced than their similarities. In Oslo one is shown the writing-room in which Ibsen spent the last years of his life. It contains a not very flattering portrait of Strindberg. Ibsen is supposed to have referred to him as his 'master'. That assessment of their rival skills is not the usual one and Strindberg did not return the compliment.

Ibsen's plays are self-sufficient. It isn't necessary to know much about Ibsen's life to see what he is getting at. Yet his almost monastic reticence is so striking that one is all the more tempted to try to say something about the man behind the side-whiskers.

Strindberg's plays on the other hand are intensely subjective and in some cases incomprehensible to anyone not knowing the profound emotional eruptions behind their composition.

Ibsen then was born in 1828 in the small timber town of Skien in the south of Norway where his grandfather had settled. When he was four his father's extravagance led to poverty and disgrace. Many of his plays are coloured by domestic gloom.

In due course he took a job as a chemist's assistant in the

tiny town of Grimstad. In his spare time he studied for university entrance but he was a lonely boy and devoted many hours to painting and reading in solitude thus acquiring an independence and an ability to concentrate which remained with him throughout his life. It was perhaps by way of compensation, as the psychologists say, that he turned to writing plays. His response to the tumultuous events of 1848 was to write a play about the Roman conspiracy and attempted revolution of Catiline. In 1850, aged twenty-two, he went to Christiania, the capital of Norway, now rechristened Oslo, persisted in his studies, did some writing, and burnt his fingers in revolutionary politics.

Though he was a poet of some ability he seems already to have realised his ambitions as a dramatist, for he sought and secured a job as dramatic author attached to the Norwegian theatre in Bergen, a lively project in a lively little town. This courageous venture was dedicated to the creation of a Norwegian national drama to help displace the Danish influence that was dominating Norwegian culture. (In politics it was the Swedish influence the Norwegians were trying to shake off.) This passion for Norwegian nationalism led to Ibsen's interest in folklore and history. We can see how he used this material in his early historical dramas and in *Peer Gynt*.

During five and a half years at Bergen he was involved in staging—in the capacity of coach, assistant-stage-manager, and designer—one-hundred-and-forty-five plays. Nine of these plays were by the prolific and competent French dramatist Eugène Scribe, whose thorough-going methods of constructing plays made a deep impression on the young Ibsen and influenced his subsequent technique.

While he was at Bergen, Ibsen set himself seriously to the task of writing plays. He was a young man living in a country that was making its first strides towards cultural independence and it is not surprising that his first plays should have been written in the mood of European romanticism. It is extremely interesting to compare *Lady Inger of Ostrat* (1855) and *Gildet paa Solhaug* (*The Feast at Solhaug*, 1855) with *Goetz* and *Egmont*. Neither were successful with the public though they are impressively powerful plays to read; but the latter won the critical approval of one of the most distinguished of his young contemporaries, Bjornstjerne Bjornson.

To the personal friendship and critical support of Bjornson Ibsen owed a great deal. Bjornson had a fresh international outlook, considerable facility as a dramatist, and an open nature. Ibsen had none of these things. Yet Bjornson's plays, admirable enough in many ways, have none of the penetration of Ibsen's. The quarrel, or misunderstanding that kept them apart for many years shows the worse side of Ibsen's irascible nature.

In 1857 Ibsen moved from Bergen to Christiania to become artistic director of the Mollergate Theatre. In addition to his regular duties he continued his sequence of historical plays with *Haermaendene paa Helgeland* (*The Vikings at Helgeland*, 1858), and his magnificent *Kongsemnerne* (*The Pretenders*). It was also at this time that he wrote a five-act comedy in verse called *Kjaerlighedens komedie* (*Love's Comedy*). It was the first of his plays to create a rumpus. Critics say that it looks forward to the type of play that was to make him famous. This is true of its theme which is the delightfully shocking proposal that people who are deeply in love should never get married. But in form it's a play of his youth, with quickly flowing verse and a chorus of women whom he uses as if they were now in an Athenian comedy and now a modern American musical.

His work in Christiania came to an end in 1864. He was thirty-six. None of his plays had been a marked success and there was a good deal of hostility to his ideas. It was a time of political tension in Norway and Ibsen was disgusted at his country's attitude to the growing power of Germany. Having been awarded a small scholarship by the government he left

1
Performance
of *Hecuba*
by Euripides
at Epidaurus

II
Concert at
the theatre
of Herodes
Attikus

III
Theatre
of
Dionysos

IV Roman theatre at Orange, France

Monastery
of the
Escorial,
Spain

VI

A
Calderon
play at
Einsiedeln

PETRVS CORNELIVS ROTHOMAGENSIS
Anno Dñi. 1643.

VII Corneille

Edelinck Sculp. C.P.R.

VIII Racine

XI   An open-air stage in Italy

XII
Goldoni's
A Servant
of Two
Masters

XIV Goethe

XIII Schiller

XV
Goethe
at the
court at
Baden

XVI
Ibsen

XVII
Strindberg

XVIII The Ghost Sonata by Strindberg

Norway and went to Rome. Except for a couple of brief visits it was twenty-seven years before he returned.

In Rome, and on subsequent visits to Dresden and Munich, he lived in the greatest poverty. The inadequacy of the European copyright laws lost him proper payment for the revival and publication of his plays, and he refused any form of literary compromise simply to make money. With a concentration that was both stubborn and fanatical he devoted himself to the single dedicated task of writing the plays he wanted to write.

Among his next four plays there is one, *De unges forbund* (*The League of Youth*, 1869) which does look forward to his celebrated social dramas, but it is not an important work. The other three are among the great dramatic masterpieces of the world. They are *Brand*, *Peer Gynt* and *Kejser og Galilaer* (*Emperor and Galilean*). In length and sheer quality of writing they are tremendous works. *Brand* was a kind of contemporary morality about the relationship that exists between a man of inflexible ideals and his society; *Peer Gynt*, likewise a morality, surveys the whole life of a man, not an intellectual idealist, but one who seeks sensual fulfilment in the realisation of his commercial ideals; *Emperor and Galilean* is about Julian the Apostate, the Emperor who tried to combine under a single imperial order the spirit of both Christ and Plato. These three heroes represent the Christian, the materialist and the philosopher and in these plays we can see taking shape the ideas which Ibsen fully evolved in the plays of his maturity.

There can be few greater experiences in dramatic literature than to read the complete works of Ibsen chronologically right the way through to the final *Naar vi doede vaagner* (*When We Dead Awaken*).

And while it may be true that Ibsen's mind does not roam as widely as Schiller's did, no dramatist has ever developed his view of life with such concentration, or sharpened his technique in the process with such growing assurance.

I am not qualified to judge the verse which Ibsen used in *Brand* and *Peer Gynt*, but the severity with which certain critics attacked the language of these two plays determined him thereafter to write in prose, which was certainly more in keeping with his purpose.

In 1870, long before he had finished *Emperor and Galilean* there occurred an event which made a great impression on him. This was the Franco-Prussian war which culminated in 1871 in the destruction of the French army and the siege and occupation of Paris. Ibsen wrote from Dresden, where he was then living, to the distinguished Danish critic George Brandes that the Prussians had put paid to the revolutionary ideas of the eighteenth century (liberty, equality, fraternity, and all that) and that now there was needed a revolution in the spirit of man.

And this is precisely what he set about to achieve himself. He finished *Emperor and Galilean*, moved to Munich and wrote nothing for four years. Then he received two excellent plays from Bjornson, *Redaktoren* (*The Editor*) and *En fallit* (*A Bankruptcy*, 1874) and he entered upon a tremendous phase of creative writing with the social dramas on which his fame is based.

Between 1875 and 1882 he completed at roughly two yearly intervals and in this order *Samfundets stotter* (*The Pillars of Society*), *Et dukkehjem* (*A Doll's House*), *Gengangere* (*Ghosts*), and *En folke fiende* (*An Enemy of the People*). These fine plays present few difficulties to reader or audience. They deal in general terms with social problems. *A Doll's House* has become celebrated for its powerful assertion of women's rights. *Ghosts* is perhaps the only masterpiece ever to have been written on the subject of venereal disease. Bernard Shaw made a collection of the critical abuse with which this play was received on its first production in London. *An Enemy of the People* deals with the social problem of bureaucratic dishonesty in a small community. These plays made Ibsen even more hated and feared than before he left Norway. But the number of his supporters was growing fast.

Ibsen was now faced with the problem of evolving a theatrical technique that would do justice to the growing maturity of his ideas. Finding that to thrust deeply into the nature of human beings limits increasingly the possible scope for physical action, he developed a technique that had been admirably demonstrated by Sophokles in *Oedipus*. The action of a play begins at a certain point of time, near the climax in the relationship of two people. The action is advanced not by further action, but by the continual revelation of past actions. Thus the classical unity of the situation is preserved with all its intense concentration upon the emotional crisis of the protagonists, the events leading up to the crisis are revealed, and the action is led up to the moment of disaster.

From this point in his career Ibsen developed a further device. This was a vocabulary of dramatic symbols by which the inner thoughts and feelings of his characters could be exteriorised. In *The Wild Duck* we have the little attic which represents the remote and unreal world of Ekdal and his family; in *The Lady from the Sea* we have the restless longings of an unsatisfied woman symbolised in continual references to the eternal movement of the ocean; and in *Rosmersholm* the mill-race at the bottom of the garden represents the violent new passions that have been unleashed in the house with all their destructive fury. Tarnished and bleached by scores of lesser imitators symbolism is at the moment out of fashion; but there is a very strong case to be made that the very nature of drama, the exteriorisation of an idea in terms of human action, is symbolic.

And so as Ibsen's interests moved from the social world of men to the inner world of man, he became increasingly concerned with the struggle of man with his own false values, a corrupt reflection of a corrupt society. The theme of *The Wild Duck* is the destruction of the stuffed and stuffy dream-world of Hjalmar Ekdal and his family by the brutal realism of Gregers Werle. In fact the theme of self-destruction runs through a number of his plays. We see the self-destruction of Hedda Gabler in pursuit of ideals without the sense of reality to give them conviction; of Rebecca West in *Rosmersholm* who refused to face her own guilty past; the problem of Alfred Allmers in *Little Eyolf* who bereft of his book, his child, and the love of his wife and the woman he loves is at last obliged to face the reality of his situation or be destroyed.

So it comes about that Ibsen is described as the supreme enemy of the idealist and his fellow the sentimentalist. Yet though insisting upon the ultimate destruction of so many of his heroes and heroines through their refusal to face the reality of the world they are living in, it should not be thought that Ibsen is a writer of dreary stories and destructive philosophy. Of all dramatists he is in many ways the dramatist of youth. His heroes and heroines are usually men and women of boundless energy. Brand, the younger Peer Gynt, and Julian have the romantic verve of Goetz and the intellectual passion of Faust. They thrust to the frontiers of human experience, Brand of religious experience, Peer Gynt of sensual experience, Julian of political experience. Halvard Solness destroys himself climbing to the pinnacle of a building at the insistence of a girl. *When We Dead Awaken* ends with the artist and his former model climbing up a mountain to their death rather than descend to eternal mediocrity and safety; and John Gabriel Borkman is a great industrialist, with the world at his feet, wrecked by his own false illusions. In this sense there is a heroic quality in Ibsen's protagonists.

It is hardly surprising that a man who throughout a long life analysed with increasing penetration the nature of intellectual passion should have rebelled against the spiritual poverty of the middle classes who were playing an increasingly dominant and ineffectual role in European affairs. Romantic socialism of the 1789 and 1848 varieties came for him to a violent end in the Paris Commune in 1871. There was no longer any hope in politics. Nor in religion. An ethical revolution was needed in the soul of man.

Thus there is no question of Ibsen having been a socialist. Neither by instinct nor conviction had he any wish to be involved in politics. 'I do not believe in the emancipatory powers of political measures nor have I much confidence in the altruism and good will of those in power', he wrote, and asked continually whether it was a good thing that politics should continue to take such precedence over social problems. In 1884 he wrote, 'Since *The Wild Duck* deals neither with the Supreme Court, nor the right of absolute veto, nor even with the removal of the sign of union from the Norwegian flag (burning questions of the hour to his countrymen) it can hardly be expected to arouse much interest in Norway.'

At the same time the violence of his views on social matters convinced many people, especially after the production of *Ghosts*, that there was no kind of anarchist, demon, or Satan in disguise that was not lurking behind those enormous whiskers. After the appearance of *Ghosts* he was in fact branded as 'an enemy of society'. His sardonic answer was to write a play with this very title. *An Enemy of the People* makes a scathing attack upon the vested interests of majorities who will smother the truth rather than risk their status. After this play there were people who claimed that far from being a socialist Ibsen was an enemy of democracy. His purpose in fact is very simply stated in a letter he wrote in 1890. He was speaking of *Hedda Gabler*. 'I wanted to depict human beings and human destinies upon a groundwork of certain of the social conditions and principles of the present day.'

Throughout the twenty-seven years in which he lived in voluntary exile he became not so much a lonely as a supremely independent figure. His coat-tails became longer, his side-whiskers bushier, his habitual expression more taciturn. He abhorred literary parties and artistic cliques. He was personally unattractive, short of stature, and accustomed to walk with little short steps. He conducted his life with scrupulous regularity to the last detail.

Though his plays are shot through and through with imagery, symbolism and a strong undertow of mysticism, and though he meditated upon each play upwards of two years before he set pen to paper, he was stern and business-like in all his affairs. Yet he was an abominable letter-writer and a poor speaker. He enjoyed the minor pleasures of life and was devoted to his wife and child, a boy who grew up to marry Bjornson's daughter. At the age of sixty he had a flutter with a young actress and made admirable use of the experience in *The Master Builder*.

His stature as a dramatist exceeds that of any other writer in the nineteenth century. All his plays are readable except perhaps the early histories which are rather involved. (I exclude *The Pretenders* which is a most powerful and impressive play.) It's probably true to say that they both caused and furthered a revolution in the theatre. In 1887, midstream in Ibsen's career, André Antoine founded in Paris le Théâtre Libre expressly for the production of naturalistic and social plays by writers like Zola and Ibsen. In the next few years similar theatres, mostly designated Free or Independent, were founded in many European cities; and Ibsen's plays formed a substantial part of their repertory.

This new movement in the theatre was caused by the inability of the commercial theatres to handle the new social drama, quite apart from the disinclination of the managers to do so. Ibsen, Strindberg, and Chekhov needed new methods of acting and production. The men who evolved these methods were André Antoine, Otto Brahm in Germany, Harley Granville Barker in England, and of course Constantin Stanislavsky.

Ibsen's European reputation can be seen in the simultaneous publication of *Hedda Gabler* (1890) in New York, London,

Paris, Copenhagen, Stockholm, Christiania, Berlin, Leipzig, St. Petersburg and Moscow.

While it's interesting to know something of the personality that glowers behind those tremendous plays, it is quite essential to know something of the life of August Strindberg. No more subjective dramatist has ever lived.

August Strindberg (1849-1912) was twenty-one years younger than Ibsen. He was the child of ill-matched parents who had eight children and went bankrupt. Intensely sensitive, prone to tears, loathing school but full of curiosity, he adored his mother who died when he was thirteen and resented his father's immediate marriage to his housekeeper. (A classical background for an emotionally unstable person.) Moody, brooding and difficult, incapable of concentrating on any job for long, throughout adolescence he was a misery to himself and others. Though in due course he began to scratch a poor living as a teacher and tutor, a profound restlessness prevented him attaching himself permanently to a steady job. In time he turned to the theatre, failed as an actor, tried his hand at writing plays. He drew upon a wide range of subjects, religion, philosophy, free thought. None was successful. He threw up the theatre and turned to journalism. Back to acting. Then back to journalism. He suffered the while from a rancorous sensuality; he needed desperately the friendship of a woman, yet he was unable to make any lasting friendships. He was twenty-six when he fell properly in love, and then it was with a married woman who happened also to be an actress, though owing what little success she had more to her beauty than her talent. Her name was Siri von Essen.

In 1877 he married Siri and for a number of years they were happy. *Master Olaf*, a play he had written some years previously was successfully produced; he wrote his children's fairy play, *Lucky Peter's Travels* and his answer to *A Doll's House—Herr Bengt's Wife*. Strindberg did not care for Ibsen's so-called emancipated women. And then the marriage took an inevitable turn for the worse. Their doctor advised a trip to Paris. Though he still had had no success as a dramatist he was not lacking literary admirers. He enjoyed the friendship of Bjornson, of the distinguished Danish critic Georg Brandes, and in time, of the great philosopher Friedrich Nietzche himself. Finding no serenity in Paris they moved to Switzerland where Strindberg brought out a book of stories called *Married* which depicted some of the hatreds and tensions of his life with Siri. The book became a fashionable shocker like *Ghosts* which had also just appeared. In Sweden Strindberg was prosecuted for blasphemy. He returned to Stockholm and conducted his own defence, seeing himself as a heroic figure like Ibsen's Brand defending the rights of free speech and personal integrity.

By this time his marriage with Siri had assumed nightmare qualities. Although there were times when he loved her devotedly he was continually torn by jealousy, hatred, and every emotion of an excited and unbalanced mind. It was in this mood that he wrote his first dramatic masterpiece, *Fadren* (*The Father*, 1887). This, the most straightforward of his plays is about a Captain who embodies many of his own profound anxieties: doubt as to the paternity of his child, doubt as to his own sanity, intolerable relationships with his wife. He followed this fine play a year later with *Fröken Julie* (*Miss Julie*, 1888), the gruesome tale of an affair between a degenerate aristocratic girl and her father's valet.

Both these plays were staged by Antoine who helped Strindberg to realise the dramatic possibilities of the one-act play. Caught up by a new enthusiasm and envisaging the creation of a theatre entirely devoted to the production of his own plays he quickly wrote *Fordringsägare* (*Creditors*), a psychological masterpiece which he considered himself to be among his best works, *Paria*, *Simum*, and *Den starkare* (*The Stronger*). The last of these plays is perhaps the most widely performed of all his works for it touches upon the sexual attitudes of women towards men in the most subtle manner, while it shows considerable originality in its construction. Consisting of a duologue between two women, only one of them speaks, and it is the silent one, so it appears by the end of the play, who is the more powerful of the two.

Unhappily for Strindberg the theatre which had been opened in Copenhagen collapsed along with his marriage. He went to Sweden in 1891 and divorced Siri. For a time he retained his capacity to write and around the year 1893 produced a collection of one-act plays which all deal in a penetrating manner with some aspect of sexual relationships. We are not so well off for one-act plays that this fascinating group can properly remain without the benefit of a competent translation. Their titles are: *Debet och kredit* (*Debit and Credit*), *Första varningen* (*First Warning*), *Infor döden* (*Facing Death*), a very moving little play, *Leka med elden* (*Playing with Fire*), very well worked out, *Moders kärlek* (*Mother Love*), and *Bandet* (*The Link* or *Bond*).

Separation from Siri left Strindberg 'tormented by conflicting emotions' and it was in this mood that he made his second marriage, this time to a young Austrian journalist named Frida Uhl. It was even more disastrous than the first and lasted less than a year. The success of *The Father* which had been staged in Paris for the second time took Strindberg once again to France but the years between 1894 and 1896 were the years he afterwards referred to as his Inferno. His interest in chemistry and physics was growing. He lived as a recluse, charred his fingers making chemical experiments, took up alchemy, delved in the occult and black magic; was at various times in prison, in hospital; always refusing friendship, refusing charity. For a time, to be blunt, he was mad. The loyalty of his friends, especially Frida's mother, the philosophy of Swedenborg, and the promises of the Catholic Church, brought him back to sanity. (He never actually became a Catholic.)

In 1898 he returned to Sweden and to something approaching normal life, and set to work on a new group of plays, less subjective but by no means the least significant part of his output. The best known of these plays are *Folkunga-sagen* (*The Volsunga Saga*, 1899), *Gustav Adolf* (*Gustavus Adolphus*, 1900) and *Eric XIV*.

Then there are the tremendous plays in which he continued to work out the sexual problems he had first described in *The Father*. *Brott och brott* (*Crime and Crime*, 1899) deals with the death of his first child and the sense of guilt it left him with. In *Dödsdansen* (*The Dance of Death*, 1901) his mood is more enveloping. The subject is the relationships of a couple who have been married for twenty-five years, who live in a granite fortress in inescapable proximity to each other, who detest each other, but are unable to leave each other until the woman succeeds in killing the man, not with anything so crude as a knife or poison, but with sheer malice of mind. This play has led many people to describe Strindberg as the supreme misogynist. This is a very superficial view. Strindberg was violently critical of women, ready to expose and describe every little weakness in them, not because he detested them but because he adored them, because he was unable to establish satisfactory relationships with them, because they thwarted him. Anyone who had hated women would not have cared as Strindberg cares. In this sense *The Dance of Death* is perhaps his masterpiece.

He then ventured into marriage for the third time. His choice was Harriet Bosse, a fresh and beautiful young actress. Again their relationship petered out after a couple of years but not before it had led Strindberg to write some of the most original of all his plays. He was preoccupied with mortality, with personal difficulties, with failure. But far from submitting he makes a prodigious attempt to discover a kind of freedom, to shake off the futility of carnal things. *Till Damaskus* (*To Damascus*, 1898-1904), *Advent* and *Ett drömspel* (*The Dream Play*, 1902) are not easy to understand for they are shot through with, and compounded out of a great variety of highly personal religious and mystical experiences, as well as the influence of contemporary philosophers, notably Nietzche and Swedenborg. *Pask* (*Easter*, 1901) and *Svanvit* (*Swanwhite*, 1902), both written for Harriet Bosse are very much easier. The former is an exquisite piece of writing.

Meanwhile the experience of André Antoine's little theatre in Paris in the eighteen-eighties had remained in his mind as the ideal milieu for the intimate and personal plays he now wanted to write. When he heard that the great German producer Max Reinhardt had opened a Chamber Theatre (Kammerspiel) in Berlin he lamented once again the absence of such a theatre in Stockholm where his own plays could be produced. A young actor-producer named Augustus Falk came forward with a practical scheme and the means to carry it out and on November 26th, 1907 a Strindberg Theatre was opened in Stockholm. Unfortunately it was as unsuccessful as other seasons of his plays had been. But this is hardly surprising when we consider the plays he wrote to be performed there. These chamber plays as he called them, *Ovader* (*The Storm*), *Brande Tomtem* (*After the Fire*), and *Spöksonaten* (*The Spook* or *Ghost Sonata*) are masterpieces of their kind but it is a difficult kind, very personal and not likely to interest more than an extremely small and specialised audience. And in this case it is not disparagement either of the plays or of audiences. Indeed I am afraid that we are brought up against one of the limitations of dramatic art. Strindberg's Chamber plays are to a large extent what we should call 'surrealist'. They are compounded of intensely personal symbols which were clearly of enormous portent and significance to Strindberg himself but which are inevitably remote from audiences who do not share his own particular imaginative life. The general content of the plays is clear enough: they are about the inner life of man. *After the Fire* shows us the burnt-out ruins of a house. The residents come poking about among the charred remains and are reminded in the cupboards and crannies that are now disclosed of secret thoughts, intuitions, memories and fears that have likewise remained concealed until this moment. *The Ghost Sonata* is about a group of people from whom Strindberg has stripped the masks of their identity, leaving them like so many boney skeletons. He likewise reveals the house piecemeal, its secrets and its secret life. It's a fascinating idea. But having reduced a group of characters to bare bones, skeletons, or sets of nerves, he has to find theatrical terms in which he can express these characters. To do so he relies upon his own personal esoteric symbols. Sometimes they are explicable to an audience. More often not. The plays remain little masterpieces of their kind and an enormous challenge to enterprising producers, but not a body of drama upon which a permanent theatre can be founded.

It will by now be clear that in the course of his life Strindberg experimented with a great variety of theatrical forms. Nothing however will be gained by listing a series of -isms. It is enough to say that there is a strong element in his various plays of all the most powerful movements in European art and literature of his day. He wrote naturalistic plays of the kind that had been produced in Paris by Zola and Antoine, he wrote plays that were full of the new discoveries in psychology that were shortly to be given to the world by such men as Sigmund Freud. He wrote plays that were responsive to the mystical philosophy of the Swedenborgians and other plays that were a kind of dramatic version of the impressionist movement in painting. In all these experiments he was clear what he was trying to do and explicit in his objective. Here, for example, is a revealing passage from the preface to *Miss Julie* which explains the apparent formlessness of some of his earlier plays.

The preface is a fascinating piece of dramatic criticism which tells us a very great deal about Strindberg's aims and the theatre of his period.

'I have avoided the mathematically symmetrical construction of French dialogue and let people's brains work irregularly, as they do in actual life, where no topic of conversation is drained to the dregs, but one brain receives haphazard from the other a cog to engage with. Consequently, my dialogue too wanders about, providing itself in the earlier scenes with material which is afterwards worked up, admitted, repeated, developed and built up, like the theme of a musical composition.'

This Preface is full of similar fascinating comments. One begins to understand the fitful elusive quality of much of Strindberg's dialogue—even in translation—so much less taut, less substantial than Ibsen's owing to his wholly different aims.

I want to quote another passage, this time not from Strindberg but from the Belgian poet and dramatist, Maurice Maeterlinck, whose delicate atmospheric plays have something in common with the later plays of Strindberg. Strindberg indeed came very much under the influence of Maeterlinck and found great pleasure in a book of essays, mostly on mystical subjects, called *The Treasure of the Humble*. One of these essays is called *The Tragical in Daily Life*. Maeterlinck begins by saying—

'There is a tragic element in everyday life that is far more real and penetrating and akin to our true self than the tragedy that lies in great adventure . . . and this essential tragic quality comprises more than that which is merely material or psychological. Its province is to reveal to us how truly wonderful is the mere act of living. . . .' and here we get to the point. 'Is it beyond the pale to suggest that the real tragic element in life, normal, deep-rooted and universal, only begins at the moment when so-called adventures, sorrows, and dangers have disappeared? Is the arm of happiness not longer than that of sorrow, and do not certain of its attributes draw nearer to the soul? Must we indeed roar like the Atrides before the eternal God will reveal himself to us? and is he never by our side at times when the air is calm and the lamp burns on unflickering? Indeed when I go to the theatre I feel as though I were spending a few hours with my ancestors who conceived life as something primitive, arid, brutal. . . . What can I learn from creatures who have no time to live because there is a rival, or a mistress whom they are obliged to put to death? I have grown to believe that an old man sitting in his armchair, giving unconscious ear to all the eternal laws that reign in his house, interpreting without comprehending the silence of doors and windows and the quivering voice of the night . . . I have grown to believe that he lives in reality a deeper, more human and more universal life than the lover who strangles his mistress, the captain who conquers in battle, or the husband who avenges his honour.'

I believe that this describes what Strindberg was often trying to do.

BOOKS FOR FURTHER READING:

All Ibsen's plays have been adequately translated. The standard version is that of William Archer but there are many alternatives. Translators on the whole avoid the most interesting *When We Dead Awaken* which Archer tackles splendidly; but I do not think his version of *Love's Comedy* is as satisfactory as the version in Everyman.

There are Lives and critical works on Ibsen by Edmund Gosse, Janko Lavrin, M. C. Bradbrook, and Brian Downs.

The historic critical analysis of Ibsen's plays is of course

Bernard Shaw's *Quintessence of Ibsenism* which is included in *Major Critical Essays* in his *Collected Works*.

Strindberg has been best treated by the Germans who have for long had a complete translation of his plays and have staged them even more frequently than the Swedes. As a result of translations by Elizabeth Sprigge, Peter Watts and Max Faber the situation is improving. But there are still many fine plays waiting for a definitive rendering.

The best biographies are by Elizabeth Sprigge, and Brita Mortensen and Harold Downs in collaboration.

Married to Genius is an account of his second marriage by Frida Strindberg. Though unattractively written it includes a lot of fascinating material especially about Strindberg's visit to England in the summer of 1893.

A translation of three of Bjornson's comedies is available in Everyman.

There is a tendency to think that Ibsen has drawn a fairly accurate picture of bourgeois life in Norway with its domestic tensions and tragedies set in a land of eternal rain, misty mountains and dank fjords. It's therefore worth pointing out that Ibsen's characters are transportable to any other part of Europe; and that today the Norwegians are as gay a people as are to be met in the world. Far and away the most profound and successful production of *Peer Gynt* I have seen was in Oslo directed by the late Hans Jacob Nielsen who also played the leading part.

In this connection it occurs to me that because Strindberg was a neurotic we are inclined to think that his work is not typical of Sweden. I have not visited the country myself but I have been impressed by the extraordinary similarity of imagery in the plays of Strindberg and the marvellous films of Ingmar Bergman, particularly *The Seventh Seal* and *Wild Strawberries*.

CHAPTER TEN

The Russian Dramatists:
Chekhov and his Contemporaries

ANTON CHEKHOV was born in 1860. He was thus rather younger than Ibsen, whose plays he disliked intensely, and a contemporary of Strindberg for whom, surprisingly, he had a considerable respect. It's difficult to imagine three men more dissimilar than the remote and dedicated Ibsen, the sensual and unbalanced Strindberg, and the sensitive, ironical, and rather lovable character of Chekhov. Yet when we consider their plays together, what a magnificent start they give to the drama of the twentieth century! It's not surprising that their imitators have been legion, that few techniques have been developed in the course of the present century which weren't foreshadowed by one of them, and that in performance their plays still strike us as extraordinarily fresh and undated.

Chekhov became an adult at a difficult time for a Russian writer. There was no vigorous literary movement with which he could identify himself. The recent past had been notable; but in 1881, the year he celebrated his twenty-first birthday, Dostoievsky had died, and two years later Turgenev. Count Leo Tolstoy had passed his greatest creative period and was now the Grand Old Man of Russian letters and a revolutionary pamphleteer. It is not surprising that he was the greatest literary influence in the life of the young Chekhov. There were no other giants.

In the theatre conditions were even more unsatisfactory. Until 1881 Russian theatres had been limited to those receiving a licence from the government (or Czar), exactly as happened in London until the Theatres Act of 1843. Thus in Moscow there were only three theatres, the Bolshoi (large) theatre, the Maly (small) theatre, and a summer theatre in a park.

The Maly was the more important having staged the works of Russia's greatest dramatists, Lermontov, Griboyedov, and Gogol, notably the latter's famous plays *Revisor* (*The Inspector General* or *Government Inspector*, 1836) and *Zhenitba* (*Marriage*, 1847). (And what splendid comedies they are!) This had been due not so much to the enterprise of the management as the insistence of some of the greatest actors the Russian stage has produced, men like Mochalov, Karatygin, and Shchepkin who envisaged before anyone else in Europe the possibilities of a kind of realism in acting which was not finally realised until the end of the century.

Shchepkin was at his prime in the eighteen-forties. During the next decade the most notable figure in the Maly was the dramatist Alexander Ostrovsky (1823-1886) who had an ideal interpreter of his plays in the actor Prov Sadovsky. Ostrovsky has in fact become identified with the Maly and his statue still stands in the square outside the theatre. Though an honoured name in Russia he has never made his mark in this country. He wrote forty-three plays and made a number of translations. I have read eight (in English) with keen pleasure. He was an exponent of the kind of realism which Chekhov was to develop, using not so much a story as a theme around which he weaves a succession of scenes of Russian life, closely observed and rich in characterisation. When he develops a tighter story as in *The Storm* he is closer to Turgenev of *A Month in the Country* (1850) than to Chekhov. A play such as *The Ward* is not among the world's supreme masterpieces, but it should be widely known for the wholly underivative and beautifully observed manner in which it has been written.

These magnificent writers were living in a country that was ruled by Czars who one after the other announced their belief in autocracy and their disgust with liberalism. This inept political structure was supported by secret police and savage censorship of literature, the press, and the theatre. Yet even in the eighteen-eighties grumbling was turning into action. Revolutionary cells were being formed. The first principles of dialectical materialism were being discussed. The origins of the Bolshevik party, which was to take power in 1917, had been established. This was the background against which the young Chekhov began to write his highly successful stories.

Anton Chekhov was born on 16th January, 1860, in the town of Taganrog on the Sea of Azov in south Russia. His father, who kept a shop for the sale of groceries and quack medicines, was eccentric. He had six children of whom Anton was the third. Holding strict religious views he organised his children into a choir, marching them to church at all times of day and night and in all weathers. He was an erratic disciplinarian and made free use of the stick. Chekhov had an unhappy childhood. His life became a little more endurable when in his teens he discovered a passion for the theatre and a talent for acting and writing. The title of his first play suggests a certain originality of outlook, *Not for Nothing did the Chicken Stammer*.

When he was sixteen his father went bankrupt and the home broke up. His father and mother went independently to Moscow. Anton stayed on in Taganrog to finish his education; but visiting his mother in Moscow and seeing the poverty in which she was living he decided that he must take up a profession which would enable him to keep her properly. He therefore decided to become a doctor. And so in 1879, at the age of nineteen, he joined the rest of his family in their almost intolerable squalor.

He faced his divided responsibilities with enormous energy. There were his university studies and the need to make as big a contribution as he could to the disastrous finances of the family. To earn money he cultivated his talent for writing humorous short stories and articles. He was successful in both capacities. By 1884 he had passed his degree in medicine and began to practise as a doctor, and by 1887, when he was still only twenty-eight, he had become a celebrated young writer with six hundred stories to his credit. More than this he had a host of friends and an enormous zest for life. He also had an incurable tuberculosis, though he does not seem to have realised or admitted the nature of his illness for some years.

Yet his gregariousness was remarkable. He adored people, and was unable to resist inviting almost everyone he met, irrespective of class, creed, or colour, to come and stay with him. Wherever he happened to be living, his house, his flat, his room, was a scene of continual coming and going. And this tremendous sympathy for, and penetrating understanding of human beings emerges in his glorious stories. Here are no judgments, no shaking of the finger, no frenetic outbursts of emotion, but a gay and ironical revelation of the human scene, farcical, tragic, but never reproving.

Yet Chekhov's love of company was offset by a strong contemplative streak in his nature. He was not a person who sought to avoid his own company. Perhaps some of Chekhov's creative genius was the result of his ability to harmonise the contradictions in his nature.

It was in the year 1887 that he came under the influence of Count Leo Tolstoy who the year before had written his first play, a powerful affair called *The Powers of Darkness*. Chekhov was impressed by Tolstoy not so much as a writer but as a thinker and a doer, a man who lived his own brand of socialism, who advocated a theory of non-resistance and practised an extreme form of charity. Yet he was reluctant to meet Tolstoy. He seems to have known himself well enough to realise that his artistic strength lay in a kind of objective and dispassionate view of human nature that would be destroyed by commitment to a political programme. He was fearful of being unable to sustain his own hesitancies in front of the forceful personality of the Count. Tolstoy on his side, though anxious to meet the brilliant young story-teller, thought that Chekhov was too vague, too reluctant to commit himself, and lacked the ability to see clearly where he was going. Like many other people he demanded that Chekhov should state unequivocally where he stood politically. Here again I think that Chekhov's genius sprang from an ability to reconcile these contradictions. As a matter of fact the two did not meet until 1895. They remained good friends with much respect for each other's work, but little for their ideas.

It was also in 1887 that Chekhov again turned his attention to the theatre. He had written a number of plays but they had come to nothing. He was now asked to write a comedy by a commercial manager of the name of Korsh who was running a theatre for the entertainment of Muscovite merchants. In those days Moscow was the commercial capital of Russia and St. Petersburg, now Leningrad, its cultural centre. Chekhov was a natural choice to an enterprising manager for he was the most gifted and amusing story-writer of the day and continually in need of money.

After a great deal of badgering Chekhov agreed. He laid aside his first novel which was giving him a lot of trouble, and wrote *Ivanov* in ten days. History does not relate what Korsh thought of the manuscript. Perhaps he didn't think anything for it was a considerable scoop to be able to display Chekhov's name on the posters. *Ivanov* is a curious blend of tragedy and comedy, full of strokes of brilliance and 'typically Chekhov'.

Chekhov attended rehearsals and quarrelled with the actors.

He was not naturally irascible but even at the age of twenty-seven he seems to have had a clear idea of how he wanted his plays acted and the customary four rehearsals were ridiculously inadequate for actors to come to terms with a play far different from anything they had ever come across before. Chekhov was disgusted with the performance but the play was reasonably successful with the public and he was sufficiently encouraged to rewrite it. A year later it was successfully revived in St. Petersburg and then in Moscow.

The Wood Demon, which he wrote next in the year 1889 is another curious play, full of immaturities as we might rather portentously say, but showing further signs of his rare theatrical vision. Unhappily it was a lamentable failure and he was discouraged from further attempts at playwriting.

What Chekhov needed, as many another young playwright has done, was a man of the theatre, deeply sympathetic and himself an artist, who could help him with general problems of construction. It's not difficult to find reasons for the failure of *The Wood Demon*. Chekhov's originality lies in his total rejection of the well-knit stories of well-made plays with their coincidences and improbabilities and theatrical situations so typical of the drama of the nineteenth century. He is the first dramatist to attempt to dramatise the inner life of his characters, and to discover a way of expressing that living stillness and eloquent silence of which Maeterlinck wrote. The difficulty of rejecting the strong and proven qualities of dramatic art is to know what to replace them with if the play is to have sufficient tension to hold an audience. *The Wood Demon* is hesitant and uncertain. The emotional harmonics and overtones with which Chekhov seeks to express the reality of his characters are confused and blurred. The play lacks the incision, penetration, and sustained atmosphere of revelation that replaces a strong and coherent story, and acted with even greater uncertainty it must have seemed extraordinarily feeble to audiences who did not know what to expect. He uses none of the technical devices which Ibsen developed, but relied, as often as not, on silence.

There was one aspect of the theatre in which Chekhov was supremely successful. Korsh, like all commercial managers of the nineteenth century, was accustomed to round off the main play of the evening with a short vaudeville or farce in one-act which would send the audience away happy. In spite of the failure of *Ivanov* Korsh persuaded Chekhov to try his hand at this genre. Between 1887 and 1897 Chekhov wrote a group of delightful one-act comedies *Medved* (*The Bear*), *Predlozhenie* (*The Proposal*), *Tragic ponevole* (*A Tragedian in spite of Himself* or *An Unwilling Martyr*), *Svadba* (*The Wedding*), and *Yubiley* (*The Anniversary* or *A Jubilee*). There is the assurance of a master in these little plays.

In spite of the fact that Chekhov was accustomed to disparage everything, it is not surprising that he should have dismissed them. Since they were financially successful he could afford to dismiss them—but they were simply not what he was trying to do. Chekhov's excellent biographers set out a number of problems that were on his mind in the year 1890. He felt the need to recreate himself as a writer of short stories. His letters make clear that he felt himself in danger of getting into a treadmill and repeating himself. He wanted to resolve the conflict that Tolstoy had set up in him. He had become emotionally involved with a woman from whom he wanted to escape. And although there is no evidence for this it is probable that he was deeply concerned about his future as a dramatist.

The upshot of these many anxieties was that he undertook an arduous and dangerous trip to the penal settlement of Sakhalin in the far north of Siberia, returned by ship, and shortly afterwards set out on a European tour that took in Austria, Italy, and France.

Everything we know about Chekhov emphasises the inconsistencies in his character. He was a wonderful raconteur, he loved to play practical jokes, as a host he was never content until his place was crammed with guests; yet he is continually brooding upon his incompetence, his poverty, his responsibilities; we see him living like a recluse, unwilling to meet anybody and unable to write a line. He wanted to be a do-gooder, yet he hated having to commit himself to a practical programme. He liked good food and pretty women yet he had the strongest puritanical convictions. On his return from his European tour he bought a house and estate at Melikhovo, some fifty miles from Moscow, where he established his family. For the rest of his life his illness and the theatre took charge of him.

In 1895 Chekhov turned again to the theatre and wrote *The Seagull*. He had not been asked, prodded, or invited; he was not in desperate need of money; he wrote the play because he wanted to. His letters give no indication of what was passing through his mind but one has the feeling that he must have suddenly seen his way, how to do it. For *The Seagull* is a masterpiece; and I think he must have felt that he had got somewhere near what he was aiming at for he took the unusual step of reading it aloud to a group of his friends. Their reaction must have been a grave disappointment. They were unable to make head or tail of it. He sent it to a young friend of his, a playwright named Vladimir Nemirovitch-Dantschenko, and even visited him to hear his judgment. Dantschenko gave Chekhov a long, sympathetic, and appreciative criticism, finally suggesting that after revision the play should be sent to the Maly Theatre. Chekhov produced a letter from the leading actor who had already read the play advising him to give up writing for the theatre since his talents clearly did not lie in that direction.

Nevertheless he was encouraged by Dantschenko's criticisms and after revising the play sent it to his friend and publisher Suvorin enclosing a note in which he expressed his utter lack of confidence as a dramatist. Suvorin, who had enormous respect for Chekhov's talent, took the play with him to St. Petersburg and offered it to the Imperial Alexandrinsky Theatre.

The play was accepted and in the autumn of 1896 was put into production. The whole affair was disastrous. The Alexandrinsky was a gold-and-plush theatre where middle-class audiences went to enjoy broad farce and bustling melodrama. The play was hopelessly under-rehearsed and the actors were all at sea. The first performance began with titters and ended with jeers. Chekhov's humiliation was completed by the dramatic critics who said the play was not simply bad but idiotic. He swore he would never write another play.

He returned to Melikhovo and then took a holiday in France. He wrote more stories. Two years went by. He then received a letter from Nemirovitch-Dantschenko announcing that he and Canstantin Stanislavsky had founded a People's Art Theatre and asking permission to include *The Seagull* in the repertory of their first season.

In view of the prodigious failure of the play in St. Petersburg this was a bold move on the part of Dantschenko and Chekhov needed a good deal of persuading. In fact he never gave his whole-hearted approval.

The first season of the Moscow Art Theatre, as the venture came to be called, opened on October 14th, 1898. Plays by Tolstoy, Shakespeare, Hauptmann, and Andreiev had nothing like the success that was needed to keep the theatre open. The future of the enterprise depended upon *The Seagull*, a play that had already flopped. The company was on edge and Chekhov pessimistic.

It is well known how the first performance turned out to be one of the great events in theatrical history. At the end of the first act the applause broke out with what Dantschenko described as a 'deafening crash'.

Chekhov's four masterpieces have always been closely identified with the Moscow Art Theatre. Yet there is some doubt whether the company did succeed in realising the spirit of these marvellous plays. Stanislavsky's ultimate achievement as a producer has placed him above criticism. But Chekhov himself was always emphatic that neither as producer nor actor did Stanislavsky properly realise what they were all about. Briefly the early productions of the Moscow Art Theatre were too gloomy, too theatrical, too preoccupied with a kind of fussy naturalism. Stanislavsky's productions were extremely effective—but in the wrong way.

Chekhov has been severely criticised for sending his next play to the Maly although he knew that Dantschenko was eager to have it. But when the Maly asked for extensive altera-tions Chekhov bristled and sent the play to Dantschenko.

The new play *Diadia Vania* (*Uncle Vania*), a rewritten and much improved version of *The Wood Demon*, was only moderately successful. The company was in despair. Only Chekhov was unmoved. By this time he was without illusions about the theatre.

But his health was worsening. He had been obliged to leave Melikhovo and take a house near Yalta in the congenial atmosphere of the Crimea. He was in poor health and low spirits; but a new play was germinating in his mind. Dants-chenko realised that he could only be sure of securing it for the Arts Theatre if he gave Chekhov a chance to see his own plays in performance. He therefore arranged to take the com-pany to the Crimea the following summer. They opened at Sevastopol with *Uncle Vania*. Chekhov was in the audience. On the second night he enjoyed a performance of *The Lonely* by the German dramatist Gerhardt Hauptmann; on the third the company gave *Hedda Gabler*. Chekhov hated Ibsen and spent the performance in the dressing-rooms. He did not attend the performance of *The Seagull* on the fourth night. Stanislavsky's misinterpretation of Trigorin cut very deep.

But he was sufficiently impressed with the production of *Uncle Vania* and in particular with the spirit of the company

to promise them his next play. The company returned to
Moscow and Chekhov settled down to write *The Three Sisters*.
The play gave him continual difficulty. 'I am writing a play
with four heroines', he wrote in a typically caustic vein. But
it isn't difficult to see the problems he set himself, or the concentration that was needed to maintain a clear dramatic line
in a play that is composed, almost like a fugue of half-a-
dozen themes playing in and out of each other, yet always
supplementing, continuing, and developing each other. And
throughout the arduous period of composition Stanislavsky
was urging Chekhov to 'get on with it' as the company needed
the play for immediate production.

Chekhov finished *The Three Sisters* in October and showed
something of his personal concern for the play by taking it to
Moscow in person. He stayed on for rehearsals, but at the first
reading he sensed that neither Stanislavsky nor Nemirovitch-
Dantschenko, far less any of the actors, had the least idea of
what the play was about or how it should be acted. He had a
furious row with Stanislavsky in his hotel, left Moscow, and
made no further attempts to explain his intentions or to put
the company right.

The play was staged on January 31st, 1901. It had a luke-
warm success and only came to be recognised as a masterpiece in the course of time.

A complete and disastrous break between the best dramatist
and the best company in Russia was only avoided by a
fortunate accident. In the May following the production of
The Three Sisters Chekhov married the company's leading
lady, Olga Knipper. It was to prove a curious courtship after a
curious marriage, with Chekhov spending most of his time in
Yalta and Olga Knipper, a devoted and enthusiastic member
of the company, rehearsing and playing in Moscow.

But there was no longer any question of him giving his
next play to anybody else. In the autumn of 1902 he went
again to Moscow and actually conducted some rehearsals of

The Three Sisters evidently to the advantage of the production. On his return to the south his wife rarely ceased importuning him for the new comedy which he had promised and which the increasing strain of his illness made it always more difficult for him to write.

Vishnevii sad (*The Cherry Orchard*) was not staged until January 17th, 1904. Chekhov remained with the company throughout rehearsals, trying to make the producers understand that the play was a comedy and not a bourgeois tragedy. Stanislavsky and Dantschenko seem to have been reluctant to accept his argument. Chekhov was now too ill to argue and let them have their way.

Six months after the production of *The Cherry Orchard* Chekhov died in Germany. He was forty-four. *The Seagull* was the only one of his plays which he had seen achieve an outstanding success. A seagull has become the emblem of the Arts Theatre. But that does not give us the right to foster a legend that Chekhov was the victim of continual and wanton misunderstandings. It is quite impossible at this distance of time to make a valid critical estimation of those first productions of Stanislavsky. What is important is that Stanislavsky and Nemirovitch-Dantschenko together created the finest and most lasting theatrical ensemble the western world has ever seen—with the possible exception of the Comédie Française. More than this—they went on to show the world, perhaps not how to produce Chekhov, for that would be to produce an absolute standard that would be destructive of creative art, but how to approach the production of Chekhov which is a very much richer legacy. The artistic truth that is crystallised in what is rather unfortunately known as 'the Stanislavsky method' is one of the great contributions to the theatre of the twentieth century. Their own original productions of Chekhov may not have been very good. We don't know. It's hard to say. Anyway it doesn't matter. But they got somewhere near it, they continued to get nearer still, and they made it possible for producers all over the world to find their way towards the heart of this most lovable of all dramatists.

I sometimes wonder whether the universality of Chekhov is not one of the strangest of theatrical phenomena. Chekhov peopled his plays with characters who had failed. All are frustrated, disappointed, out of step with time and circumstance. They do not seek to realise some great ideal as Ibsen's do, they do not tear each other asunder like Strindberg's neurotic protagonists. He does not show us men and women in the grip of an overwhelming passion in the romantic manner or the victims of fate in the classical fashion. His characters are very ordinary Russian men and women depicted with such truth and sympathy and perception that we see in them some of the absolute and universal qualities of human nature. I am sure that Chekhov's insistence on his plays being comedies is important, not to prove that the Art Theatre was wrong but because it was Chekhov's way of insisting upon the irresistible ebullience of the life-force. I have spoken of the dichotomy of his nature, how he was both gregarious and a recluse. These two sides of his nature are clearly demonstrated in his life. A Soviet critic has summed up his achievements like this:

'When he died he left behind him not only twenty volumes of universally famous prose, but four village schools, a high-road to Lopasnya, a library for an entire city, a monument to Peter I, a belfry, a forest which he had planted on waste-land, and two wonderful gardens.'

That is why the underlying spirit of his plays is an affirmation of life and not an acceptance of disaster.

BOOKS FOR FURTHER READING:

Chekhov has been admirably served by biographers. The most detailed life is David Magarshack's *Chekhov*, the most technicoloured Princess Nina Andronikova Toumanova's

Anton Chekhov, the Voice of Twilight Russia, and Irene Nemirovsky's *A Life of Chekhov,* my favourite Ronald Hingley's *Chekhov.*

William Gerhardi's *Anton Chekhov* is a useful critical study of his methods and philosophy.

On the plays alone I recommend David Magarshack's *Chekhov the Dramatist,* but it's fair to point out that in the overall perspective of European literature many critics think his stories represent a greater achievement than his plays.

An extremely interesting example of the new Soviet 'line' on Chekhov is provided by Kornei Chukovsky's *Chekhov the Man,* which seeks to destroy the twilight legend and turn him into a gay and robust social worker without a touch of the recluse or the introvert.

There are several admirable selections from his voluminous and highly readable correspondence, particularly, *The Selected Letters of Anton Chekhov* edited by Lilian Hellman, 1955 and *Letters of Antan Chekhov to his Family and Friends* translated by Constance Garnett.

Essential to understanding Chekhov the dramatist are the two great books on the Moscow Art Theatre, Stanislavsky's *My Life in Art,* and Nemirovitch-Dantschenko *My life in the Russian Theatre.* Stanislavsky in his ebullient theatrical manner betrays his rather superficial attitude to Chekhov even to letting slip his enthusiasm for incidental sound effects, one of the gimmicks which infuriated Chekhov and which were not always well handled in the impressive visit of the Moscow Art Theatre to London in the summer of 1958.

These two books, together with Joseph Macleod's *Actors Cross the Volga* have a good deal to say about Maxim Gorki, a dramatist of great significance to the Russian theatre but whose European standing is not yet established.

The story of the first production of *The Seagull* is told in full in my own *Great Moments in the Theatre* and Stanislavsky's production notes have also been published.

CHAPTER ELEVEN

European Masters of the Twentieth Century

W HO THEN ARE the masters of the twentieth century? I
have excluded writers of our own country since I dealt
with them in my book *Masters of British Drama*.

It is not likely that many people will want to dispute the
names of the dramatists that have been included. Some may
be surprised at the honour accorded Mercadé and Gréban but
it is clear that in the past these writers have not been given
adequate recognition. Others will question Gozzi's right to be
included, but it is impossible to understand Goldoni without
knowing something about his rival. (And how the irascible
writer of scenarios will hate to look down from the Elysian
Fields and see that once again he is playing second fiddle to a
dramatist!) No one is likely to question the omission of Voltaire; but more might very well have been said about the
enchanting plays of Marivaux, supreme among the lesser
masters.

The list of possible claimants is considerable. There is much
to admire in Ludvig Holberg, the eighteenth century Danish
dramatist; in Gotthold Lessing, his German contemporary;
and particularly in Beaumarchais who in a couple of enchanting comedies, *Le Barbier de Seville* (1775) and *Le Marriage de
Figaro* (1784) created Figaro, a timeless and unforgettable
character.

During the first half of the nineteenth century there was an important group of German dramatists which included Friedrich Hebbel and Heinrich von Kleist. Two of Kleist's plays have been successfully revived in recent years, *Der zerbrochene Krug* (*The Broken Jug*, 1808), and *Der Prinz von Homburg*, (1810). The greatest of German romantic dramatists was Richard Wagner. Since he spent a large part of his life trying to create a new form of art he called 'music-drama' and thereby complete the experiments begun by Goethe and Schiller, he would have had no objection to being included among the masters of dramatic art; but it's for his music that his operas are performed.

In nineteenth century France the catalogue of distinguished dramatists becomes impressive. From Marivaux to Sardou the list includes Victor Hugo, Alfred de Vigny, Alexandre Dumas father and son, Eugène Scribe, Emile Augier, and the important naturalistic writers like the Goncourt brothers who fell in behind the leader of the movement, Emile Zola. At the end of the century we find another distinguished group in Germany —Gerhardt Hauptmann, Hermann Sudermann, and the curious Franz Wedekind. And Spaniards will rightly insist upon proper respect being paid to Jacinto Benavente.

Comparison can help to clarify the qualities of a supreme master. He is not always the most able dramatist. Sardou was an incomparably better technician than Goethe. But Goethe had something to say and Sardou didn't. He wrote some magnificent roles for the great Sarah Bernhardt but one expects a master, in Zola's phrase, to present a moment in the conscience of mankind. A dramatist without a mind or a pen of distinction maintains his status by the sheer actability of his plays. The truth is that we look for a certain demonism in the master. His work is a challenge. His life is a quest. That is why we are often interested to watch a master functioning below his best, Schiller in *Don Carlos*, for example, or Strindberg in his dream plays, great men feeling towards an individual creative style, illuminating as they do so the nature, the variety and even the limitations of dramatic art; and also, in many cases, clarifying the spirit of their period, as Gréban enshrined the spirit of the later Middle Ages in his *Passion* and Shakespeare crystallised the Renaissance. In the same way Ibsen, Strindberg, and Chekhov expressed quite clearly a prevalent European mood, a kind of fin- or mal-de-siècle, a strange malaise that descended upon the continent in the latter part of the nineteenth century and which unfortunately seems to have come to stay.

And so we come to our own troubled times.

It is no accident that Ibsen, Strindberg, and Chekhov explored in their plays what might be called the inner life of man, the nature of his personality, his many emotional conflicts, his social attitudes, his relationships with other people. They lived at a time when a new branch of science was being revealed. The study of psychology has given us a new understanding of human nature. Sigmund Freud, Alfred Adler and C. G. Jung are among the undisputed giants of the age. Even sensational advances in the sphere of nuclear physics have not lessened the importance of recent discoveries in psychology, physiology and neurology.

Elementary psychology has proved a blessing for dramatists of the twentieth century, especially the less gifted or inventive ones. It has provided them with a rich new vein of high quality and easily workable ore. Unfortunately few of them have had outstanding creative genius either as writers or thinkers—and it's doubtful whether the two functions can be separated—to fashion it into anything beyond what was achieved by Ibsen and Chekhov. It's difficult to think of a so-called psychological drama that does not fall badly short of Strindberg's tremendous play, *The Dance of Death*. Indeed the outstanding dramatists of the century have in few cases made capital out of psychological discoveries though the whole drama of the period has been tinged with recognition of this new field of study.

The only European dramatist to have entered profoundly into the world of the mind is the Italian, Luigi Pirandello, and while he is a most able and gifted dramatist who explored a field of human experience that had never before been touched, no one would call him a great original thinker. Having discovered a subject that proved to be highly suitable for dramatisation, namely the nature of reality, he plays with it like a juggler who can keep a large number of Indian clubs in the air at once. Yet he is not a glib or superficial dramatist but a highly professional technician who took the trouble to construct his plays firmly, to create living characters, and to develop his material in an individual and entertaining manner. That in the course of doing so he did not explore the fastnesses of the human soul is only to say that the great creative genius is a rare phenomenon.

Here is a passage from one of his letters in which he gives some interesting facts about his early life.

I was born in Sicily, at Agrigentum, 28th June, 1867. At eighteen I left Sicily to go to Rome. But a year later I departed for Germany where I stayed a year and a half. I took my degree at the University of Bonn with a thesis written in German. From Bonn I returned to Rome . . . bringing Goethe with me. I then taught for twenty-four years in a school for young girls, from my thirtieth to my fifty-fourth year. . . .

Excellent, but Pirandello omits the crucial fact. As a young man he married a Sicilian girl who was beautiful but what we should call 'extremely difficult'. After six fairly happy years she began to show signs of a serious mental breakdown. At first her neurosis took the form of an intense jealousy towards the girls whom Pirandello taught—as well she might for he was both handsome and exceedingly clever. She began to tyrannize over his life. In his own words, he became the plaything of a mad woman, a martyr to imaginary crimes. Early in the first World War his eldest son was captured by the Germans. His second son fell ill with tuberculosis. His daughter was driven mad by the jealousy of her mother who insisted the girl was going to poison her, and attempted suicide.

Pirandello was now forty-three. For twenty years he had lived the life that Strindberg depicts in *The Dance of Death*. It was only then that he put his wife in a mental home.

Now the many stories that Pirandello wrote as a young man suggest that he had always been interested in the oddities of illusion and delusion even before his wife's psychosis made them a part of his daily life. However much he suffered during those twenty years of domestic anguish the artist in him remained sufficiently detached to store up this mass of hardly endured experience. He did not forget or suppress it: he used it.

In 1917, in his fiftieth year, he began to turn his attention seriously towards the drama. During the next twenty years he wrote thirty-seven plays, remarkable studies all of them in paranoia, delusion, the nature of reality, and the curious world of twilight that hovers between the often dreary and meaningless actions of daily life and that remote and only half recognised world of the mind that suddenly erupts in flashes of reality more real than the chair you are sitting on. These plays include some of the masterpieces of European drama— *Sei personaggi in cerca d'autore* (*Six Characters in Search of an Author*, 1921), *Enrico IV*, (*Henry IV*, 1922), *Così è se vi pare* (usually translated *Right You Are if You Think So*, 1917), and *La vita che ti diedi* (*The Life I Gave You*, 1923).

Pirandello was fortunate in finding those ideal interpreters on which to a certain extent every dramatist, even the most gifted and creative, depends, to bring his work to final resolution on the stage. These were Ruggero Ruggieri and the actress Marta Abba in Italy, and that magnificent couple Ludmilla and Georges Pitoëff in France. It is curious that his plays have not held the stage more consistently in Britain. The absence of anything approaching a standard translation of his major plays is an example of this. There do not even exist the linguistic problems such as torment the translator of Racine.

Now one of the greatest problems facing a dramatist, particularly in his early plays, is that of the convention within which he is going to write. Every artist is naturally obliged to face problems of form. With the dramatist it's a peculiarly difficult problem because although in one sense his material is literary, his play is something that is written down, it does not end with the completion of the script like a novel or a poem. Indeed the real difficulties and complications only begin when the manuscript is seized by agent, manager, producer, actor, musician, designer, carpenter and stage-manager who have to get together to create a composite work of art that will be appreciated by a large public.

There are a very large number of ways to write a play. That need not be emphasised to anyone who has read straight through this book. The *Oresteia* of Aeschylus, Gréban's *Passion*, Racine's *Phèdre*, Ibsen's *Peer Gynt* and Strindberg's *The Ghost Sonata* are all so different in every detail that it is difficult to find any common principle except that they provide actors with parts. In practice, of course, it's often a little easier than it sounds. The dramatist who is not an innovator writes like he sees other people writing. Arnold Wesker, for example, writes naturalistic plays of the kind that have been written for half-a-century. He admits to having no interest whatsoever in theatrical form. This is not to imply that his plays are good or bad but that in the form in which he writes them they are unexceptional.

Other dramatists are worried about form. The naturalistic convention does not suit the kind of play they want to write. Robert Bolt clearly had to do a good deal of thinking before he arrived at the form in which he wrote *A Man for all Seasons*.

He was obliged to face the fact that he couldn't say what he wanted to say about Sir Thomas More in the same form he had used for *Flowering Cherry*.

The naturalistic convention in which most plays have been written and are being written in the course of the twentieth century depends upon the curtain going up on a scene that looks like, or is intended to look like, a room with one of the walls taken away. Some producers and designers take a great deal of trouble to make their interiors look convincingly naturalistic; sometimes they aim at a ridiculous and most unconvincing glossiness, sometimes their efforts are simply dull. But this usually depends upon the whim, the ability, or the technical and economic resources of the producer and his designer and not upon the playwright.

The playwright is usually aware that an interior setting is a somewhat cumbersome affair and that if he wants to avoid excessively long intervals in his plays, as well as the virtual certainty that his plays will never be presented, he must try to avoid shifting the action too often from one interior to another, especially if they are complicated interiors with a stairscase and ceiling and things.

This leads the playwright who is using a naturalistic convention to limit his action to as few different scenes as possible. To the modern playwright this is a practical expedient which he will understand and accept even though it may cause him extreme difficulties in constructing his plays and account for some of the absurdities that we see in the work of the less skilful. But to dramatists like Racine, what was called in the seventeenth century 'unity of time, place and action' was a canon that had to be observed. He couldn't write like Hardy if he wanted to, for his plays would quite simply have been jeered off the stage. He was therefore obliged to concentrate his action into a single place whether he wanted to or not.

As it happened this concentration was particularly suitable

for the plays that such dramatists as Racine wanted to write, plays which depicted a group of heroic characters reaching some moment of crisis in their life. It was also a suitable one for Ibsen in his later plays. It suited Strindberg in plays like *Creditors*, *The Father* or *The Dance of Death* when again he wanted to demonstrate a group of characters passionately turned in upon themselves. But it didn't suit Ibsen when he wanted to show the life of a man, as in *Peer Gynt*, or a man wrestling with a religious problem as in *Brand*, or two men wrestling with even greater problems as in *Emperor and Galilean*. So in these plays Ibsen used another convention, a form of writing far closer to that of Mercadé and Gréban than to Racine.

We find Strindberg evidently making the same choice. When he takes as his subject not a group of people at a moment of crisis but a man or a group of people going through some experience over a period of time, as in *Advent* or *To Damascus*, like Ibsen, he breaks away from what we might call the classical form and uses the Shakespearian or medieval.

By examining plays in this way we can see that by and large two dominant traditions have emerged in the European theatre, so far as theatrical form is concerned, the classical and the medieval. We can also see that to a certain extent each is rather more suitable to a certain kind of theme: the classical lends itself to personal crises, the medieval to narrative; the classical to a central situation, the medieval to a series of situations; the classical to personal problems, the medieval to man in relationship to social, political, or religious problems that are outside himself.

In the mid-twentieth century the dominant style of writing is still the classical though a growing number of attempts are being made by dramatists, not to write in the medieval convention—it's not as easy as that—but to find a form that will enable them to write with greater responsiveness to the tremendous problems of the world. The criticism that is usually made of the dominating naturalistic convention is its triviality and pettiness. Naturally enough. A dramatist who commits himself to a form that is ideally suited to depicting a group of people at a moment of crisis, and lacks the skill and passion to present a crisis, will simply present a group of people fiddling around with trivialities. Many French dramatists, aware of the predicament, and the recipients of an intense classical education, have gone back to Greek sources for their material. Cocteau, Anouilh, Neveux, Sartre, Gide, Claudel, Montherlant, Giraudoux and Obey, without going farther afield, have all, in recent years, adapted, translated, or dramatised a Greek play or myth. Splendid though many of these plays have been they tell us little other than the rather obvious fact that the truths enshrouded in Greek myths are as relevant today as ever. Far and away the most significant of the dramatists who have faced this problem seems to me to be Paul Claudel.

Claudel, having received a classical education, was converted to Catholicism in Notre Dame de Paris on Christmas Eve, 1886, when he was eighteen years old.

Between 1889 and 1898 he wrote a group of plays that show his preoccupation with classical form and Catholic thought. On the one hand he made a translation of the *Oresteia* and wrote two versions of the remarkable *Tête d'or*, an interesting but not altogether successful attempt to create a kind of romantic mythology set in a classical mould; on the other he wrote *Le Repos du septième jour* in which Catholic content is compressed into classical form, and the first draft of the splendid *L'Annonce faite à Marie* which eventually turned out to be one of the most successful Catholic plays of our time. Somewhere between the two kinds of work there is *La Ville* (two versions, neither wholly successful) and the splendid *L'Echange*, a play of such power, precision, and psychological interest that I am astonished it should never have been performed in England.

In this sectarian and divided world of ours many people are inclined to dismiss Claudel for his passionate Catholicism. To such people it is both a strength and a weakness of Claudel that he should be less of a thinker than a visionary; and for this he is probably the better dramatist. For the drama seems to be better suited to the presentation of visions, or of a world that has been seen and created by a dramatist, than to argument and discussion. Claudel uses the classic form a good deal in his early plays in order to give stature to his human beings. But having created them and shaped them he does not set them in opposition to the Almighty as Aeschylus does: he places them in front of the Almighty. He presents the human predicament in Catholic terms and leaves it at that.

Others resent his spate of words. French critics complain that he wrote French as if he were writing German. It's a part of the same problem. He is concerned by the confusion and uncertainty of human thought and feeling. He finds that human life is bedraggled with indecision, irresolution, doubt, and ignorance. He tries to express all this in his language. The woofly texture of his lines is a part of the woofly texture of human thought. If we feel that he overwrites it's partly because so many other dramatists have underwritten.

This is all evident in his masterpiece, *Partage de Midi* (1905), a play about three men and a woman who in the full heat of noon and at a climax in their lives, play out their passions in the sight of God, without understanding themselves, the people they are speaking to, or the God they are attempting to serve. The play has a Shakespearian richness of texture.

Between 1909 and 1916 he wrote the final version of *L'Annonce faite à Marie* (*The Tidings Brought to Mary*), and another magnificent presentation of a Christian predicament in *L'Otage*. This play is particularly memorable for the matured and richly developed character of Berthe.

Between 1919 and 1924 he wrote *Le Soulier de satin* (*The Satin Slipper*). The significance of this play in the development of Claudel is not in its thought, which is uninteresting, but in his reversion to the medieval form. His subject is no longer a group of people bound together in critical relationship such as he depicted in *L'Echange*, *L'Otage* and *Partage de Midi*, but a picture of Christendom at the time of the Spanish Renaissance and of the vast complex working-out of human destinies in a Catholic world. In its original form the play was intended to be presented on four separate evenings like a medieval Mystery. It remained unperformed until in 1943 Jean-Louis Barrault made a shortened version of it and staged it with enormous success in front of an audience that included leading members of the German General Staff at the Comédie Française.

Claudel's last play, *Le Livre de Cristoph Colomb*, though not perhaps his most successful work of art, is by far his most interesting play. Roughly, the subject is similar to that of *Le Soulier de satin*, with Columbus the hero of a great Catholic adventure. The play is written almost medieval fashion, in a number of short scenes, the action shifting continuously between Spain, the ship and the Indies. The whole thing is knitted together by means of various technical devices of which the most striking is a continuous use of chorus.

The explanation of this important exploration of a new theatrical form lies in Claudel's professional career as a French ambassador, in which capacity he spent many years in Tokyo. This gave him wide experience of the marvellous classical theatre of Japan and the more popular Kabouki, both of which employ highly conventional stage forms and considerable use of music. Claudel has left an informative analysis of the place of music in the theatre in the Preface to the published version of *Le Livre de Christoph Colomb*, a memorable piece of dramatic criticism.

The so-called naturalistic revolution in the theatre can be traced back to the middle of the nineteenth century. In England it can be dated fairly exactly from Squire Bancroft's pro-

ductions of Tom Robertson's plays at the Prince of Wales
Theatre in the eighteen-sixties. That's to say, we have had
sitting-rooms and kitchens looking very similar to real sitting-
rooms and kitchens for close on a hundred years. On the basis
of longevity alone it is not surprising that some dramatists
should be looking for other theatrical forms, and particularly
those more susceptible to expressing the spirit of the times.
While dramatists have found a great deal to admire in the
medieval and Shakespearian drama, producers have turned to
the theatre of Japan and China which in their classical form
were, and are, even more highly conventionalised. To discuss
this in greater detail would take us into the province of
theatrical history; but it is interesting that two of the most
significant dramatists of the century Paul Claudel and Bertolt
Brecht, should both have found inspiration in the theatre of
the Far East.

In order to explain the rather curious similarity between the
two men, here are a few facts about the life of Brecht.

Brecht, born at Augsburg in Bavaria, was the dramatist
of Germany in crisis. He came to manhood at a time of
national disaster. His first plays, *Baal*, produced in 1919 when
he was twenty-one, and *Trömmeln in die Nacht* (*Drums in the
Night*, 1920), are full of the agony and despair of a defeated
Germany and the country's political collapse. He came to
Berlin and was associated with the work of the communist
producer Irwin Piscator who in his 'Politischer Theater' was
staging a succession of plays of urgent didacticism, swingeing
satire, and uncompromising socialism. His methods of staging
were revolutionary and totally a-naturalistic. Under the inspiration of Piscator, the young Brecht wrote a number of
highly didactic pieces—'lehrstücke' he called them—treating
his themes from a socialist point of view. The form that he
used is broadly speaking medieval. *Die Ausnahme und die
Regel* (*The Exception and the Rule*, 1930), for instance, begins
'I am the merchant Karl Langmann and I am on my way to

Ourga to conduct a piece of business'. This is very reminiscent of the famous opening of the Chester play of *The Deluge*—

I God that all the world have wrought. . . .

In a naturalistic play a character cannot simply turn to the audience and announce who he is : that wouldn't be natural. So the dramatist has to spend a lot of time and technical dexterity in making his identity clear in the course of some very 'natural' dialogue.

Die Massnahme (*The Expedient*, 1930) is about four communists who seek to justify a certain course of action, namely the killing of one of their number, by acting out their crime in front of a jury who in the play performs as the chorus. Played in London in the early nineteen-thirties with music by Hanns Eisler, this curious play turned out to be a memorable piece of theatrical pleading. Brecht used the chorus in very much the same way as Claudel uses it in *Christoph Colomb*.

In his early satires such as *Aufstieg und Fall der Stadt Mahagonny* (*Splendour and Decadence of the Town of Mahagonny*, 1927) and the famous *Die Dreigroschenoper* (*The Three Farthings* (or *Threepenny*) *Opera*, 1928) he collaborated with the composer Kurt Weill to enrich and point his political satire.

The upshot of many years of experiment, of trying to create a drama responsive to the political movements of his times and of a furious frustration caused by many years of exile, was that Brecht developed a formidable body of theory. He described the style of theatre he was trying to create as 'epic', a term that has tended to create a certain bewilderment among his supporters and derision from his enemies. It's an interesting term because it's one that Aristotle used to describe the kind of dramatic poetry that wasn't tragedy, an altogether lesser form, as it seemed to him, since it dealt with ordinary characters in narrative form instead of idealised characters in dramatic form. But this perhaps is the very direction in which drama is tending to develop in the second half of the twentieth century.

But for all his theories, significant and helpful, or tiresome and distracting though they may be, in some of his later plays he achieved a synthesis between his subject and the form of expression that places them among the masterpieces of the century. Most critics agree about the outstanding quality of *Mutter Courage und ihre Kinder* (*Mother Courage and her Children*, 1938), *Leben des Galilei* (*Life of Galileo*, 1938), *Der gute Mensch von Sezuan* (*The Good Woman of Sezuan*, 1939) and *Das kaukasische Kreidekreis* (*The Caucasian Chalk Circle*, 1945).

Brecht is not perhaps the greatest dramatist mentioned in this book: his verse is often flat and his material crude; but in some ways he is the most interesting. Up to the time of his exile he was more communist than the communists, though never, he declared, himself a member of the Party. Indeed, one of his most powerful plays, *Die Massnahme* (*The Expedient* or *The Measures Taken*), has been virtually suppressed in the Soviet Union. On his return from exile he took out an Austrian passport, a Swiss banking account, gave the publication rights of his plays to a West German publisher, and accepted an invitation to live in the Communist state of East Germany, the German Democratic Republic. Here he created the Berliner Ensemble and trained the company on principles that directly opposed those of Stanislavsky which were, and are, canonical in the U.S.S.R. So although his company achieved a European reputation he himself continued to be a thorn in the flesh of the authorities to whose cultural beliefs he refused to subscribe.

He is not a sympathetic character. He has described himself as awkward. Nor can one love his plays as one can love those of Claudel or Giraudoux. His self-imposed task was to make people think. He was a complete revolutionary. By challenging in the most vivid manner the position of the artist in a communist state he has made us all his debtor. We shall betray what Brecht worked for if we alienate his plays into a romantic world of make-believe. He meant them to make us feel uncomfortable. They do. He meant to challenge our complacency. He did. We are the richer for both experiences.

Yet how much there is in common between the work of the two men : a passionate belief in their convictions, a readiness to experiment in the most courageous manner with theatrical form, a profound interest in the oriental theatre. But at the same time what personal differences! Brecht was thin, gangly, aggressively untidy in appearance, always unshaved and with close-cropped hair. The adjectives 'sly' and 'cunning' have been applied to him. But Claudel was a professional diplomat. Here is André Gide writing in 1912 when Claudel was forty-four : 'Paul Claudel is more massive, wider than ever; he looks as if he were seen in a distorting mirror; no neck, no forehead; he looks like a power-hammer.' And then in 1925 : 'He seems to have shrunk . . . He is enormous and short. . . .' And Jean-Louis Barrault, to whom we owe the real discovery of Claudel, says : 'When he concentrates his thoughts he seems to return to the mineral earth.'

So there we have the men that count, the giants or anyway the bigger ones, possibly the more enduring ones, in some cases the innovators. This is not to deny that there is considerable pleasure to be found among the lesser men, who instead of wrestling with the limitations of their medium and doing battle with the gods, accept the world as it is and delight us with their comments, their felicities, their sense of style. These are quite properly the tradesmen of the profession, the craftsmen, excellent and indispensable in their way, but different from the great creative artists. Who among recent European dramatists has written with so sophisticated a wit and poetic a conception of his material as Jean Giraudoux among whose plays La Folle de Chaillot (The Mad Woman of Chaillot) is surely to be accounted a lesser masterpiece? Who has written with a more gracious historical style than Henri de Montherlant in a splendid piece of historical penetration like *Port-Royal?* And if I were asked quite straightforwardly who of all European dramatists writing in the nineteen-sixties possessed the greatest intellectual stature and brought to the drama the greatest intellectual authority I would name without any hesitation Jean-Paul Sartre. *Les Sequestrés d'Altone* seems to me a major contribution to the literature of guilt and social responsibility.

I have had the keenest pleasure from reading and rereading the plays that have been mentioned in this book; but when every credit has been given to the dramatist it's the success of his play in performance that really counts. The great theatrical experiences of one's life are those that achieve a complete synthesis between play and performance. He is a lucky person who has had a dozen such experiences in a lifetime. I count myself fortunate to have seen Tyrone Guthrie's production of *The Cherry Orchard* and the Moscow Art Theatre in *The Three Sisters*; the Berliner Ensemble in *Mother Courage* and the Piccolo Theatre of Milan in Strehler's production of Goldoni's *A Servant of Two Masters*. I shall never forget Jean-Louis Barrault's production of *Le Livre de Christoph Colomb* or *Le Bourgeois Gentilhomme* at the Comédie Française or Michel St. Denis's production of Obey's *Le Viol de Lucrèce* with the Compagnie des Quinze. I can remember like yesterday the evening thirty years ago when I saw Ibsen's *Ghosts* and Robert Loraine in *The Father*. I have never seen a satisfactory production of an Athenian tragedy, but I am still mortified if I come away from an evening in the theatre without feeling that I have been touched, albeit ever so lightly by the god.

BOOKS FOR FURTHER READING:

The plays of Claudel are virtually unobtainable in English. Many of Pirandello's plays have been translated but few are in print. This is not the fault of the English publishers, several of whom would be happy to do a collected edition of his plays, but of the curious attitude of Pirandello's legatees who own the copyright. Methuens are in the process of bringing out a number of volumes of Brecht's plays in translation.

There is a single biography of Pirandello in English by Walter Starkie. Claudel has not been adequately dealt with in English but is discussed briefly in a short study by Wallace Fowlie. On Brecht there are two admirable biographies, one by John Willet and the other by Martin Esslin.

The best general survey of the period is Frederick Lumley's *Trends in Twentieth Century Drama.*

By far the best way of keeping yourself informed of developments in the modern theatre is to subscribe to *World Theatre*, published by the International Theatre Institute with the assistance of UNESCO.

Notes on the Illustrations

I   The theatre at Epidauros, on the east coast of the Peloponnese, is the finest surviving theatre of the ancient world. It holds 20,000 spectators, and visitors still remark on its astonishing acoustics. It has been restored for performances by the Greek National Theatre of classical tragedy and comedy. This photo shows how many Greek and Roman theatres, far from being squashed into the middle of a city, were sited with a brilliant sense of their scenic surroundings. The situation of the theatre at Delphi, where performances are still given from time to time, is even finer.

II   Herodes Attikus was the name of a Roman-Greek who built this theatre in A.D. 160. It has been very well restored and is frequently used for performances. It is on the same side of the Akropolis, nestling under the great walls of Themistokles, as the more celebrated Theatre of Dionysos. The two theatres are a hundred or so yards apart. In ancient times they were connected by a number of shrines, of which the most important was in honour of Asklepios, the Greek god of medicine who was also honoured at Epidauros. The top of the Parthenon can just be seen. In classical times performances were given in daylight.

III   One does not always realise how moving the ruins of a beautiful building can be until one visits Athens. I have seen a strong man weep in front of the Parthenon. I myself am deeply moved to stand in the middle of this exquisitely proportioned dancing floor, the orchestra of the old theatre, almost surrounded by the gently rising levels of the auditorium. As in most Greek theatres the actors were backed by a small temple, or façade, behind the scaena (which did for a stage) and then by mountains and sea. You can see the lack of Roman sensibility in these matters by moving from the theatre of Dionysos to Herodes Attikus. There the rake of the auditorium is steeper. The stage is backed by a high stone façade. Superb, imperious, but lacking the profound understanding of the Greeks.

IV   Here we have it, a typical Roman theatre. And one longs to know exactly what plays were given in such overpowering conditions. The whole atmosphere seems to be far too solemn for Plautus and Terence and that leaves us with Seneca who never seems to have been a popular dramatist. Nor does a theatre of this design seem suitable for spectacles. Yet the Romans wouldn't have littered the coastline of the Mediterranean with these tremendous buildings if they were not to be put to regular use. It's all very mystifying.

V   San Lorenzo del Escurial is a Spanish monastery built by Philip II, the Philip of the Armada, 27 miles north-west of Madrid. It is a severe building of grey granite, exquisitely proportioned, harmonising with its arid mountainous setting. Many Spanish kings spent much of their life and were buried in the Escurial. Its majestic solemnity and isolation symbolise the Spanish monarchy of the Golden Age. The Escurial also comprises a church, a palace and a mausoleum.

VI   I was once lucky enough to see a performance of Calderon's *El gran teatro del mundo* (*The Great Theatre of the World*) played outside the monastery of Einsiedeln in Switzerland. Here is a photograph of the performance. Gréban's mystery has been played in Paris on the parvis of Notre Dame. The great English cycles are now staged from time to time. The monastery in the background of this picture was built between 1709 and 1727. The original monastery, the scene of much liturgical drama, was founded in the tenth century. It is not far distant from the yet more famous monastery of St. Gallen.

VII   Corneille was a stolid Norman, more interesting for what he wrote than what he was. There can have been little genuine understanding between Corneille and the brilliant self-seeking politician Richelieu.

VIII   One cannot be sure that Racine really looked anything like this. But it's a magnificent portrait of a sensual, spoilt, and extremely aristocratic product of the seventeenth century —and that was Racine.

IX   This famous portrait of Molière, though engraved in 1685, twelve years after his death, is accepted as an authentic likeness. It does suggest the sardonic humour, the patience, the suffering, the humanity of this great man.

X   This superb portrait is by Philippe de Champaigne who was frequently employed by the French royal family and aristocracy. It suggests Richelieu's intellectual distinction, his arrogance, perhaps his cruelty, even the narrow-mindedness and bigotry of which he was often accused and which gave him many enemies.

XI   This lovely drawing is by Canaletto whose splendid land-scapes of London in the eighteenth century have made his work very well known in England. Here we have a typical palace in the style of the Italian Renaissance with an imper-tinent little open-air stage edging up to it. Transpose the splendour of the palace into the literary tragedies of the age and the stage into the witty and satirical humanity of the Improvised Comedy and the qualities of the latter that appealed to the Italian people become evident. At the same time it's clear that no great refinement in theatrical art was possible under such conditions and it's easy to understand why Goldoni rebelled against them.

XII   *Il servitore di due padroni* (*The Servant of Two Masters*) is one of the most felicitous of Goldoni's comedies and much the best known in England. The production by Giorgio Strehler for the Piccolo Theatre of Milan is in some ways the finest production of a play I have ever seen. The movements of the actors were choreographic, their voices were orchestrated. Yet the whole thing was so fresh and spontaneous one could almost believe the whole thing was being improvised.

XIII   Here we have the big-boned Silesian features that went with the tall lanky awkward body of this intensely sensitive man.

XIV   From the next plate it's possible to get an idea of what the elegant young Goethe, the romantic poet, must have looked like in his younger days. Here we have the seer who lived to be eighty-three, the man who achieved a universality of knowledge that has been achieved by few men before or since, a man whose eyes were said to look steadily through one like the eyes of a god.

XV   The French 'salons' where authors read aloud their latest work to specially invited guests were copied wherever French culture was accepted as setting a standard for civilised society. This was very much the case in Germany. Goethe and Schiller must have been present at many scenes such as this depicting Goethe at the Court of Charles Frederick of Baden, a duchy in the extreme south-west of Germany, notable for the vitality of its artistic life.

XVI   Here is Ibsen as he became known in his own lifetime, a legendary figure of stuffy respectability who might have stepped out of one of his own grim plays.

XVII   This vivid photograph suggests all the uncomfortable charm, the neurotic instability of the young Strindberg.

XVIII   Perhaps the most successful of Strindberg's Chamber

plays is *The Ghost Sonata*. Although the characters it depicts are on the whole recognisable human beings, the skin and flesh have as it were been stripped off them so that we look at them almost as skeletons. This photograph shows a production of the play at the Schauspielhaus, Zürich, in 1953. The decor is extremely successful in catching the curious mixture of unreality and yet of intense personal revelation which is the quality of the play.

XIX   This famous picture shows what must have been a tense and difficult moment for all concerned, when Chekhov read *The Seagull* for the first time to the company of the Moscow Art Theatre. It is rather typical that Stanislavsky who for long did not understand either Chekhov or the play should be leaning almost possessively over Chekhov's shoulder, while Nemirovitch-Dantschenko, to whose perception and determination the production of the play by the company was wholly due, is standing almost out of the picture away to the left of the group.

XX   I am glad to have found a portrait of Claudel in a lighter mood, for the massive earnestness of the man suggests that he rarely smiled. Yet there are many testimonies to his sense of humour, and about his great play *Le Soulier de satin* (*The Satin Slipper*) he says himself in a letter to his close friend the composer Darius Milhaud, '[*The Satin Slipper*] will be an enormous masquerade, a mixture of tragedy, mysticism, and buffoonery which will definitely lower my reputation in the opinion of people of taste.'

XXI   Whatever similarities we may find in their dramatic aims, there can be no greater personal contrast than between Claudel and Brecht. The former was a professional diplomat, a French ambassador. Brecht was always on the side of the workers. He persistently made the worst of his personal appearance. He was skilful at always having two days growth of beard on his chin, neither more nor less. I think that in my text I should have laid greater emphasis on his ability as a poet.

He has this in common with the great Spanish poet-dramatist Federico Garcia Lorca, that both had a flair for genuinely popular poetry which they loved to sing themselves. Lorca of course turned to the peasantry, Brecht to city workers.

XXII   I have done insufficient justice to Sartre in my text. He does not immediately occur to one as a great European dramatist. Yet the author of that splendid tour-de-force *Huis clos* (usually translated in English as *Vicious Circle*), a fine political play like *Les Mains sales* (*Dirty Hands*), *Le Diable et le bon Dieu* (*Lucifer and the Lord*), a play whose passion has much in common with Claudel, and *Les Séquestrés d'Altone* (*Altona*), to name only his outstanding achievements, is not surpassed by any other living European dramatist. I have not forgotten Jean Anouilh who is a gifted and prolific writer with a fine understanding of what is theatrically effective; but his plays are the product of a talent—and none the worse for that—and not of a deep creative necessity.

Although Brecht was the son of the managing director of a paper mill he became closely associated with the working class. In his own words

> I grew up as the son
> Of well-to-do people. My parents
> Put a collar round my neck and taught me
> The habit of being waited on
> And the art of giving orders. But
> When I had grown up and looked around me
> I did not like the people of my own class . . .
> . . . And I left my own class and joined
> The common people. . . .

INDEX

Since the purpose of this book is to introduce young people to a large number of plays which I hope they will read, see, and enjoy, and not to write a work of scholarship (though I hope my facts are all accurate), I have intentionally left inconsistencies in the index. Titles of plays are included under their author when his name is known or is mentioned. Although in the text they are usually given first in their original language, followed by the usual translation (so that the reader will become familiar with the original title of the play) in the index they are mostly given in English, followed by the original title when the habits of translators leave any room for doubt. But I have listed Molière's plays under their original titles since they are so well known as to be almost universally recognised even by those who stopped French at G.C.E. The purpose of an index is not to be clever but to help the reader find the place he wants in the text as quickly as possible.

I

J

K